MODI'S WORLD

MODI'S WORLD

Expanding India's Sphere of Influence

C. RAJA MOHAN

HarperCollins *Publishers* India

The Express Group | Express Book Series

First published in hardback in India by
HarperCollins *Publishers* in 2015

HarperCollins Publishers India, Cyber City, Building 10-A, Gurugram,
Haryana-122002, India
www.harpercollins.co.in

2 4 6 8 10 9 7 5 3

Cover image: Getty Images / Bloomberg / Contributor

P-ISBN: 978-93-5177-205-7
E-ISBN: 978-93-5177-206-4

Typeset in 11.8/15.2 Garamond Premier Pro
By Saanvi Graphics Noida

Printed and bound at
MicroPrints India, New Delhi

MIX
Paper
FSC FSC® C218906

This product is made of FSC®-certified and other controlled material.

HarperCollins Publishers, Macken House, 39/40 Mayor Street
Upper, Dublin 1, D01 C9W8, Ireland

Contents

Preface

Prime Minister Narendra Damodardas Modi has surprised the nation and the world with his enthusiasm for rejuvenating India's foreign policy. There was little expectation that a provincial leader like Modi, who served as the chief minister of Gujarat for more than a decade, would make a big difference to Indian diplomacy. That he was shunned in America and Europe for his alleged role in the 2002 Gujarat riots suggested Modi as prime minister would begin with a major political handicap on the external front. During the 2014 campaign for the Lok Sabha, he had little incentive to explain his worldview or his plans for India's foreign policy. The election manifesto of the BJP, which in an unusual move had named him the party's prime ministerial candidate, offered few insights to the foreign policy priorities of the putative government led by Modi.

Yet, in the very first days in his tenure as the PM, Modi injected new dynamism into the conduct of India's external relations. As the elected leader of the first majority government in three decades, he had considerable political authority at home and generated much interest abroad. Taking full advantage of the extraordinary mandate, he warmed up to America, recast the approach to China and Pakistan, sustained the old friendship with Russia, deepened the strategic partnership with Japan and Australia, boosted India's neighbourhood policy, wooed international business leaders and reconnected with the Indian diaspora. In reviving the India story that had begun to fade in the second term of the UPA government (2009–14), he brought personal energy to Indian diplomacy not seen since the years of Rajiv Gandhi. In speaking extempore, using Hindi for public communication, deploying social media, inventing a new lexicon, and displaying personal religiosity in public, he is very different from all his predecessors. The Gujarati pragmatism that he has brought to bear on Indian diplomacy could well turn out to be his most important contribution to India's foreign policy. If taken to the logical conclusion, his determination to make diplomacy the handmaiden of India's economic advancement could help Delhi build up India's comprehensive national power, expand its traditional spheres of influence in the Indo-Pacific, and restore India's geopolitical momentum that was lost in the second term of the UPA government.

The book takes a close look at Modi's engagement with the world until early 2015. Although I cover less than a year of his tenure, there has been enough evidence to make an informed assessment of his foreign policy. *Modi's World* captures the renewed prospect of a decisive Indian transition—from a nation mired in self-doubt and ambivalent about its international role to a responsible power that is unabashed in its quest for greater strategic influence in the global arena.

The book is structured around my columns for *The Indian Express* that appeared during 2014–15. I had tracked the limited debate on foreign policy during the elections, assessed the diplomatic legacy of the decade-long UPA government and the major developments in India's foreign policy after Modi was sworn in as PM at the end of May 2014. I have done some minor editing, and organised the columns into separate chapters. Each of these chapters deals with one particular domain of policy. I have framed these columns with two book-ends—the opening and concluding chapters—that explain the setting for Modi's foreign policy and offer the first cut at understanding what promises to be a consequential moment in India's international evolution.

I owe much to Raj Kamal Jha, the Editor in Chief of *The Indian Express*, for giving me extraordinary latitude to reflect on India's foreign policy in the paper's print and web editions. This book would never have been attempted without the constant persuasion from Ambreen Khan, the chief of corporate communications at *The Indian Express*, and support from her team, especially Navin Banswal, in organising the columns into coherent chapters. It was a delight to renew my collaboration with Krishan Chopra at HarperCollins. He had published my first book, *Crossing the Rubicon: The Shaping of India's New Foreign Policy*, in 2003. My special thanks to Sanjaya Baru, Samir Saran and other friends for reviewing parts of the manuscript and offering valuable suggestions. But I alone am responsible for any errors of fact and judgement.

I am deeply indebted to my wife Nirmala and our two children, Vasudha and Prashant, whose love and indulgence have given me the time and space to pursue my interest in world affairs. This volume is for my brothers, Bhaskar and late Ramu, whose warmth and expansive generosity helped me get ahead at difficult moments.

C. Raja Mohan
New Delhi
April 2015

CHAPTER ONE

Introduction

The sweeping mandate for the right-of-centre Bharatiya Janata Party led by Narendra Modi in the 2014 general elections did not necessarily mean that there would be significant changes in India's foreign policy. The foreign policy of a large country does not change with the installation of a new government. But it does change in response to a significant redirection of domestic politics or a radical evolution of the external environment. New Delhi had that moment in 1991, when India had to cope with the collapse of the old economic order at home and the Soviet Union abroad. The changed internal economic orientation and the external imperatives, arising from the end of the Cold War, compelled India to recast its foreign policy and national security strategy.

After the tentative adaptation under P.V. Narasimha Rao and Inder Kumar Gujral, Atal Bihari Vajpayee boldly outlined a new foreign policy trajectory for India. If objective factors define the substance of foreign policy, subjective factors are of considerable consequence in the conduct of a nation's external engagement. Strong governments seize fleeting moments of opportunity that present themselves, while the weak squander them at great cost to the nation. The style and character of prime ministers and foreign ministers make a big difference to the credibility and reputation of governments and nations.

After he took charge of India at the end of May 2014, Modi has begun to put his own imprint on India's foreign policy. Not all of his moves are a departure from the foreign policy positions of the past. He is building on the incremental evolution of India's engagement with the world over the last quarter of a century and taking major initiatives of his own. The prime minister's greater clarity on India's long-term foreign policy objectives and the political will to pursue them vigorously have injected extraordinary energy into Indian diplomacy since the middle of 2014. To understand the prospects for India's international engagement under Modi, it is necessary to understand the new domestic political context generated by the 2014 general elections in India. The election of Narendra Modi as prime minister could turn out to be an important discontinuity in the evolution of Indian politics that has begun to have a significant impact on how Delhi engages the world. Although there is no way of drawing clear lines of separation in the history of any nation, I would suggest 1989–91 as years that marked an important transition in independent India's history. An examination of the two phases that had their own distinct domestic and foreign policy orientations should help put Modi's diplomacy in perspective.

The First Republic

The first era, 1947 to 1989, was defined by three characteristics: political stability rooted in the Congress; the quest for economic autarchy through state-led socialism, and a foreign policy of non-alignment. On the political front, with the brief exception of

1977–80, when a coalition of non-Congress parties ruled Delhi, India's grand old party towered over the nation. The Congress was a big tent that held together a large and diverse political coalition and continually mediated the contradictions among them. The party, in turn, was dominated by the Nehru dynasty. Of the 42 years in this era, Jawaharlal Nehru, his daughter Indira Gandhi and grandson Rajiv Gandhi ruled India for nearly 38 years. In the Nehru years the Congress enjoyed significant inner party democracy and the governments at the Centre and the states were run by tall figures that emerged out of the national movement. After Nehru, the party came under the total sway of first Indira Gandhi and then Rajiv Gandhi and lost much of its inner dynamism. Barring the 1967 election, all others in 1952, 1957, 1971, 1980, and 1984 produced massive mandates for the Congress party. The 1977 election was an overwhelming repudiation of Indira Gandhi's excesses during the Emergency.

The broad political stability at the national level was matched by a political consensus in favour of economic autarchy. If Nehru put the state in charge of the commanding heights of the economy, Indira Gandhi lent a strong populist touch. The First Republic severely circumscribed the role of private capital, downplayed the importance of trade and shunned foreign investment. Delhi steadily cut off economic links with the subcontinent and the neighbouring regions in Asia and the Indian Ocean. The brief interregnum of the Janata Party during 1977–79 did not see any change of course. In fact, it was the Janata Party that threw American companies such as IBM and Coca-Cola out of the country. The only party that contested this broad socialist consensus was the Swatantra Party that became the main opposition party in the Lok Sabha after the 1967 elections but was swept away amidst the huge popular support for Indira Gandhi in 1971. When it reinvented itself into the

Bharatiya Janata Party in 1980, the conservative Jan Sangh adopted 'Gandhian socialism' as its economic plank. It was only during Rajiv Gandhi's tenure as prime minister (1984–89) that the first tentative attempts were made to liberalise the economic system.

In the First Republic, a consensus slowly emerged in favour of non-alignment over the years. Nehru's ideas on non-alignment were challenged at both the left and right extremes as being too aligned with either the imperialist or socialist camps. As in the economic domain so in the external engagement, a streak of radicalism steadily engulfed Indian foreign policy after Nehru. In the first decade and a half, India maintained good relations with the East and West and won economic cooperation from both. After Indira Gandhi split the Congress party in 1969 and adopted left-wing populism at home, Indian foreign policy acquired a more distinctly anti-Western tone. The 1971 war to liberate Bangladesh from Pakistan saw the consolidation of India's alliance-like relationship with Soviet Russia. The US tilt towards Pakistan in the 1971 war and its sanctions against India after the 1974 nuclear test saw India's growing alienation from the United States. India's active leadership of the Third World on global issues at the Non-Aligned Movement and the 'Group of 77' added to the growing gulf between India and the West. By the late 1970s, non-alignment moved from the pursuit of an independent foreign policy to the belief that the Eastern bloc led by Russia was a natural ally of the post-colonial world.

Within the region, the wars of 1962, 1965 and 1971 lent an intractable dimension to India's conflicts with China and Pakistan. India's Raj legacy as the paramount power in the subcontinent became increasingly difficult to sustain and Delhi's approach towards its smaller neighbours was increasingly viewed as hegemonic. Indira Gandhi, after her return to power in 1980, and Rajiv Gandhi more actively sought to renew engagement with the United States and normalise relations with China and Pakistan. But multiple constraints limited the possibilities for breakthrough on any front.

From a broader perspective, the First Republic saw the steady erosion of India's relative economic weight in the international system and a loss of its historic commercial linkages in the neighbourhood. The first decade of the new republic saw India's voice heard with some attention in the international arena. Thanks to Jawaharlal Nehru's personality, India could play a larger role than its post-Partition weight could support. But the strategic choice that Nehru made in favour of a socialist economy would result in India's relative decline through the First Republic as Western Europe and Japan bounced back after the war, and parts of East Asia, including China from 1979, embarked on a high-growth path.

India's expansive foreign policy activism in the first phase masked a steady relative decline in the nation's economic weight in the region and beyond. The growing divide between India's internationalism and inward economic orientation had inevitably a negative impact on its diplomacy. Although India's sustained solidarity with the developing world won it much goodwill in Africa, Asia and Latin America, there was little material substance in India's bilateral relations with these countries. Notwithstanding India's claims of non-alignment on the global stage, Delhi found itself closer to the Soviet Union than the West on the political front and the dissipation of economic engagement with the West made matters worse. At home, despite the triumphal victories in the elections of 1980 and 1984, the Congress government was coming under greater strain as new social forces began to assert themselves. Meanwhile the old economic order was increasingly unable to deliver, and India became steadily marginal to major developments in the world. Its foreign policy was severely constrained as its diplomacy turned defensive, impractical and rejectionist. Unlike in the Nehru years, when India was seen as having the potential to tilt the global discourse and was courted by both sides of the Cold War rivals, the later years of the First Republic saw India become a self-proclaimed leader of the Third World trade union. Meanwhile the strategic community was blinded by ideological certitudes, preferred political correctness, and abandoned an analysis of the global power shifts. When Indira and Rajiv tried to inject a measure of flexibility and realism into India's foreign policy, there was much resistance from the bureaucracy and the intelligentsia.

The Second Republic

Three features marked the emergence of the Second Republic in 1989—the collapse of the Congress, the pressures to reform its ossified economic structures, and the adaptation of India's foreign policy to the new international circumstances after the Cold War. The 1989 general elections reduced the Congress to a minority in the Lok Sabha, a position from which it would not recover in the coming decades. The brief experiment of running Delhi through a coalition during 1977–79 now became the political norm. No political party until the 2014 elections would get a majority on its own in the Lok Sabha, the lower house of Parliament. The political decline of the Congress, however, was not matched by the rise of another national party. Instead, the Second Republic witnessed the emergence of strong regional parties and the mobilisation of religious and caste identities. As a result, coalitions became the new normal at the Centre. The political centralisation of the Indira years was turned on its head, as the Centre became weak and the states strong. In the series of coalitions that emerged to govern Delhi, almost every political formation had gained a share of power at the national level in one coalition or the other.

The post-1989 political coalitions had to deal with multiple challenges at the same time. At home the communal and caste polarisation was more than matched by the growing challenge of Naxalism that limited the role of the State in a large part of the country. Meanwhile there was much trouble on the nation's frontiers with the growing restiveness in the Punjab, Jammu and Kashmir, and the North-East. But the most pressing priority was the restructuring of the Indian economy. The old order was bankrupt by 1989 and the soaring oil prices during the Gulf War of 1990–91 pushed India into a serious balance of payments crisis. Amidst a new wave of economic globalisation, labelled the Washington Consensus, there was mounting external pressure on India to reorder its economy. The reforms were slow and hesitant. Unlike in China, where Deng Xiaoping forced a new national consensus in favour of reform after Mao's disastrous left turn in the Cultural Revolution, the Indian political class was not ready to own up the agenda for reforms. The strong political consensus in favour of weak economic reforms limited the pace and scope of change at home. But much credit goes to P.V. Narasimha Rao, who served as prime minister from 1991 to 1996, for providing a measure of stability and initiating reforms at a very difficult moment in India's evolution.

The economic reforms, informed by caution and executed in stealth, did indeed produce considerable change in the quarter of a century since 1991. The period saw sustained high growth levels, including a 9 per cent annual growth rate in the middle of the 2000s. The structure of the Indian economy too changed. If self-reliance and inward orientation were the prime themes of the First Republic, interdependence was now the new dominant feature. Nearly 50 per cent of the Indian economy was now linked to imports and exports by 2014. The greatest change, however, was in the perceptions, domestic and foreign, of India's long-term economic prospects. Internally, the pessimism about the nation's future was replaced by optimism and the emergence of a youthful and aspirational population. Externally, the faster economic growth changed the perception of India from a weak third world country into a potential great power. Even with modest growth rates it was assumed that India would be one of the world's largest economies and a significant military power that could alter the global balance in a variety of ways.

As its economy expanded, India recast its foreign policy. Once again, the wise but low-key leadership of Rao generated the time and space needed for India's much needed adaptation to a world of uncertainty that confronted Delhi's diplomacy. Whether it was in downplaying the legacy of non-alignment, finding ways to calm the turbulent waters of the subcontinent, re-engaging the West, salvaging ties with post-Soviet Russia, and taking a fresh look at the regions around India, including South-East Asia, Central Asia and the Middle East, Rao outlined a new foreign policy framework for the Second Republic. Rao also ducked pressures from the United States to roll back India's atomic and missile programmes and laid the basis for a nuclear breakout by the mid-1990s. Atal Bihari Vajpayee of the BJP completed the task by conducting five nuclear tests in May 1998 and declared India a nuclear weapon power.

Although the Second Republic did not discard the mantra of non-alignment and continued to pay obeisance to the NAM, neither was central to India's diplomatic preoccupations after 1989. India was increasingly focused on minilateral organisations like the G-20, BRICS (Brazil, Russia, India, China and South Africa) and IBSA (India, Brazil and South Africa) rather than the NAM and G-77.

Even more significant was the emphasis on integrating India into the Asian regional institutions like the Association of South East Asian Nations (ASEAN), the Asean Regional Forum and the East Asia Summit. Reconnecting with the extended neighbourhood became a central objective of India's foreign policy in the Second Republic. If Rao's Look East policy was the most successful of these efforts, less significant initiatives focused on improving India's economic, political and security relations with Central Asia, the Persian Gulf, the Middle East and the Indian Ocean. These efforts replaced the focus in the First Republic on grand-standing on global issues.

The Second Republic was acutely conscious of India's lost standing within the subcontinent itself. The need for resolving the accumulated problems with the neighbours became a special priority for Inder Kumar Gujral from 1996 to 1998. The Gujral Doctrine, which stated that Delhi must be more generous towards its neighbours, was pursued with even greater purposefulness by his successors, Vajpayee and Manmohan Singh. The emphasis on reintegrating the region was reflected in the attention India paid to the South Asian Association for Regional Cooperation (SAARC) and in expanding economic and security links with the neighbouring countries.

The Second Republic saw special efforts to improve ties with both Pakistan and China. Despite the expanded threat of cross-border terrorism from Pakistan since the early 1990s, successive prime ministers sought to normalise relations with Pakistan by resolving all outstanding issues, including the question of Jammu and Kashmir. If Gujral put Kashmir back on the negotiating table with Pakistan, Vajpayee defined a sustainable negotiating format. Dr Singh, in a back channel dialogue with Gen. Pervez Musharraf from 2005 to 2007, came close to signing a framework to resolve the Kashmir question. With Musharraf's losing ground in 2007 and the attack on Mumbai in November 2008 that was organised in Pakistan, it became difficult for India to pursue the normalisation of bilateral relations. There was some progress in the resolution of the long-standing boundary dispute with China when the two sides signed an agreement on the guiding principles for a settlement in 2005. But negotiations stalled on finding a mutually acceptable territorial compromise. As China's position on the border improved, thanks to its military modernisation and the transformation of its logistical infrastructure in Tibet, and India tried to catch up, the relative peace and tranquillity on the border since the late 1980s came under stress. The two sides once again focused on maintaining stability on the border rather than resolve the dispute itself.

One of the most significant foreign policy changes in the Second Republic was more intensive engagement with the West in general and the US in particular. Although Indira Gandhi and Rajiv took important steps in the 1980s to correct the tilt towards the Soviet Union and seek more cooperation with the United States, the sustained effort to transform India's great power relations unfolded in the Second Republic. India's economic growth in the reform era helped India deepen its ties to the United States, Europe and Japan. At the same time India held on to the traditional close partnership with Russia. Even as it expanded engagement with all the major powers, there were deep anxieties in Delhi about the American dominance of the international system. The fear of American intervention in Jammu and Kashmir and the concerns about American non-proliferation policies reached a peak in the late 1990s. When India sought to break out of these dilemmas by testing nuclear weapons in 1998, the US imposed sanctions and sought to promote a resolution of the Kashmir dispute. India weathered the storm by embarking on an intensive dialogue with the Clinton Administration.

George W. Bush, who took charge of the White House in 2001, was more empathetic to India's concerns, took a strategic view of the potential partnership with Delhi, and laid the foundation for a transformation of the bilateral relations. The Bush Administration de-hyphenated its relations with India and Pakistan, adopted a policy of strict neutrality on the Kashmir question, opened the door for expansive defence cooperation and took a major initiative to end the nuclear dispute with Delhi and integrate India with the global nuclear order from 2005 to 2008. Dr Singh, who seemed to echo Vajpayee's belief that India and the United States were 'natural allies', found himself unable to handle the political backlash in Delhi to a putative strategic partnership between the two countries. If an opportunistic BJP opposed the nuclear deal that it had begun to negotiate with Washington, the Left parties, who were coalition partners to the Congress during the first term of the UPA rule, made it the breaking point. The real problem, though, was within the Congress party. The president of the party, Sonia Gandhi, who set the political direction for the UPA government led by Manmohan Singh, was deeply ambivalent about a strategic partnership with the United States. Despite coming back to power with a bigger majority in 2009, the Congress seemed hesitant to advance the bilateral relations with the US. Half-baked ideas about strategic autonomy and preserving the legacy of non-alignment regained much ground and constrained India's ability to build a genuine partnership with the US.

The inability to implement the historic civil nuclear initiative became a broader symbol of the UPA government's failure to take full advantage of a rare moment of strategic opportunity that India was presented with. None of the major strategic initiatives unveiled by Dr Singh—towards the United States, China, Pakistan and Bangladesh—could be brought to fruition. The drift on the foreign policy front was more than matched by that on the economic front. Consumed by a new variant of economic populism, the UPA government presided over a slowdown in economic growth. The political paralysis at home and strategic hesitation abroad cast a shadow over the narrative of India's rise. The Congress party, which put India on the path of reforms during the difficult moments of the early 1990s, appeared hesitant to embrace a world so inviting. The decade of the UPA rule revealed once again the persistent gap between India's promise and performance and set the stage for the arrival of Modi and the beginning of what could be a third phase.

A retrospective look at the Indian diplomacy in the Second Republic presents a mixed picture. What began as incremental adjustments in response to economic crisis at home and the structural changes in the international environment acquired a measure of boldness by the late 1990s. The new experimentation was reflected in the efforts to recast India's nuclear policy, build a new relationship with the United States and the West, revitalise the approach to an extended neighbourhood, improve relations with the neighbours and increase participation in regional institutions. The acceleration of India's economic growth provided the ballast for India's new foreign policy and generated multiple diplomatic opportunities in the second decade after reforms. Major breakthroughs in the relations with the United States, China and Pakistan and possibilities for elevating India's standing in the neighbouring regions presented themselves. But India's ability to cash in on these opportunities seemed to peter out for a number of reasons. The UPA government seemed to lose nerve and the deepening fractures in domestic politics prevented the construction of a new consensus at the political and bureaucratic levels to seize the moment. On top of it, the return of populist economic policies slowed down the reforms and made India vulnerable to the global economic crisis that hit the world in 2008. On the foreign policy front, there was a renewed temptation to adopt the earlier notions of non-alignment defined in anti-Western terms, a reluctance to seize the new possibilities for economic and strategic cooperation with the United States and hesitation in resolving problems with neighbours.

A Modi Era?

The massive electoral majority that Modi won in the 2014 general elections suggested that an era was coming to an end in India's domestic politics. For some it was the dawn of the Third Republic that would help India realise its full potential as a nation. An empowered government under a strong political leadership with proven experience in administration, which did not carry the ideological burdens of the past and was unabashed about India's great power aspirations, seemed all set to unveil a new age in the nation's evolution since the middle of the 20th century. For others, though, the triumph of Modi, with his controversial political record as the chief minister of Gujarat, was a moment of foreboding. Although sections of the minority had been attracted by Modi's development agenda outlined during the 2014 elections, there were widespread fears that the new government might be departing from the nation's secular tradition and inclusive politics.

These fears seemed to come true as Hindu extremist groups began to assert themselves within the first few months of the Modi tenure and the government seemed reluctant to confront them. On the economic front too there was concern that in the name of renewing reforms, the Modi government might become a tool of the rich and powerful and set back the efforts to create a welfare state. The first nine months of the Modi government showed at once the possibilities and dangers of a possible Third Republic. If the turnaround on the economic front remained uncertain and social harmony looked precarious, Indian foreign policy seemed to benefit greatly from the new energy that Modi brought to Delhi.

By any measure, the pace and scope of India's diplomatic engagement during the first nine months of Modi was impressive. The PM travelled to eight countries—Bhutan, Brazil, Nepal, Japan, the United States, Myanmar, Australia and Fiji—and met more than 50 world leaders at home and abroad. He participated in a number of regional and global multilateral forums, including BRICS, ASEAN, and the United Nations General Assembly. Many of these meetings, especially the multilateral ones, were indeed scheduled earlier, but they gave the PM an early opportunity to connect with many leaders. That Modi had won an impressive victory in the general elections had of course significantly raised the international interest in dealing with the new Indian leader.

After a succession of ageing leaders who followed the youthful Rajiv Gandhi, Modi was a bundle of energy and a breath of fresh air for Indian diplomacy. For a novice in world politics, Modi quickly found himself at ease in his engagement with the world leaders and enthusiastic in his outreach to public audiences with businessmen, think tanks and the diaspora. In Nepal, he touched the hearts of its parliamentarians by focusing on the multiple bonds that connect the two nations and trying to remove the multiple misperceptions of Delhi that had enveloped Kathmandu. In his interaction with businessmen, Modi signalled greater commitments to undertake reforms and improve the ease of doing business in India. With policy communities, he demonstrated a new openness that was in contrast to the tentativeness that guided India's approach to most of its international interlocutors. His vigorous personal style reinforced the international optimism about India's economic and political prospects under the new government. The external affairs minister, Sushma Swaraj, summed up Modi's foreign policy activism when she told Parliament in December 2014 that Delhi 'has moved with speed and resolve, rarely seen in Indian external engagement, to rebuild our partnerships across the world. We have set new milestones and reached new frontiers in India's foreign policy. The global response has been just as unparalleled'. The Foreign Office in Delhi had no hesitation in declaring that Modi had brought forth a phase of 'breakthrough diplomacy'.

The problem is not with the tone of self-congratulation, but the serious challenges that lie ahead. While Modi has made a good impression on the world stage, there are big questions about his ability to produce the necessary structural changes at home that are critical for the transformation of India's external relations. On the economic front, the world has its fingers crossed. Not everyone is convinced that Modi's focus on improved governmental performance is enough to impart fresh momentum to the economy. There is concern at the reluctance of the government to initiate bold and inevitably controversial reforms. Modi has taken a number of steps in 2014, including the liberalisation of rules for foreign direct investment, changes in the labour law and new incentives for domestic manufacturing, simplifying the environmental clearances, reducing the difficulties of land acquisition and improving the ease of doing business. Yet his political horizon looks clouded. Like other leaders before him in the reform era, he confronts the problem of a weak domestic political consensus in favour of radical reform. While the Congress party continues to drift to the left, there is significant resistance within the BJP and the RSS against reforms. The lack of a majority in the upper house has made his task of pushing through major reforms that much harder.

Modi faces an equally daunting challenge on the prospect of maintaining domestic peace and harmony that are so critical for accelerating India's rise on the world stage. During his campaign, Modi had succeeded in softening his image as a Hindutva hardliner by focusing on the theme of economic development. He was willing to discard many of the polarising themes that the BJP had championed in the past. This helped him widen the base of the voter support for the BJP and raised the hopes that Modi can help transcend the identity politics that weakened the Second Republic and build a new political framework for unity. In his first Independence Day address on 15 August, Modi called for a moratorium on controversial issues like casteism, communalism and regionalism. But the Hindu extremist groups have been reluctant to respect that call. Whether it was sharpening the communal divide with the Muslims, forced conversions to Hinduism, attacks on churches, or imposing a religious–cultural agenda on India's education system, there has been a new assertiveness among the extremist supporters of the BJP. If tensions between the Hindu extremist groups and the religious minorities escalate, it would have an impact on India's relations with its neighbours, especially Bangladesh and Pakistan, the Muslim world and with the West where both the human rights organisations as well as religious groups are likely to mobilise public opinion against the government in Delhi. The first sign of serious international consequences came when US president Barack Obama, during his visit to India as the chief guest at the Republic Day celebrations, warned against the dangers of widening India's domestic fault lines under Modi.

While Modi's personal political appeal remains larger than that of the BJP and is a significant factor in the Indian political landscape, there is no doubt it will be dented over a period of time amidst the difficulties of meeting the extraordinary expectations that he raised during the 2014 general elections. His surprising success in the elections is compelling greater unity among the non-BJP forces. If the divisions among the political parties facilitated Modi's impressive victory in the north Indian states, greater cohesion and coordination among the other parties could limit the future of the BJP and Modi's own political effectiveness. The weakening of the Congress party too could significantly reverse the gains made by the BJP in the 2014 parliamentary elections. For example, in Delhi, the BJP had emerged as the largest single party in the 2013 elections to the state assembly and Modi magic helped the party win all the seven parliamentary seats in the province. Yet in the February 2015 assembly elections, the BJP was just reduced to three seats in a house of 70. The triumph of the populist Aam Aadmi Party was generated as much by the vanishing of the Modi magic as the significant shift of the Congress vote base, especially that of the minorities, to the AAP. This quick reversal of political fortunes is not a new phenomenon in Indian politics. In the First Republic, the massive mandates for Indira Gandhi (1971) and Rajiv Gandhi (1984) quickly evaporated amidst the turbulence of domestic politics. A single political setback could also trigger a massive political consolidation of the opposition forces and paralyse the government despite a massive majority in Parliament. If the diversity and volatility of India's politics can deflate the strongest electoral mandates, Modi will have to find a way of nurturing his primacy in the post 2014 political terrain through a framework of inclusive politics.

Modi's robust personality was also widely seen as improving the possibilities for energising the governance in Delhi that appeared to dissipate in the Second Republic. Three decades of rule by political coalitions had significantly weakened the power of the prime minister. Constant accommodation of diverse interests in the coalition and deference to special interests of states weakened the PM's space for manoeuvre across the board. Worse still, the capacity of the PM and his office to discipline various departments was severely limited by the fact that there were multiple centres of power. P.V. Narasimha Rao and Atal Bihari Vajpayee, despite their seniority and experience, faced significant difficulties in running the governments. They had to continually cope with resistance from other parties as well as their own. The problem became more acute for Manmohan Singh, given the unique arrangement between him and Sonia Gandhi. As a technocrat with no political base of his own and an 'accidental prime minister', as his media adviser in the first term of the UPA government, Sanjaya Baru, put it, Dr Singh had no authority over his cabinet colleagues who served at the pleasure of Mrs Gandhi. This in turn eroded the authority of the Prime Minister's Office over the rest of the government. Departmentalism became rampant, where every agency and ministry acted on its own and vetoed Manmohan Singh's policy directives.

Within the first weeks of taking charge, Modi asserted his authority over the cabinet and renewed the tradition of the PM dealing with the secretaries of various ministries directly. He also strengthened the oversight and follow-up of the PMO over the rest of the government. This style of governance resembles that in the First Republic when strong leaders like Indira Gandhi and Rajiv Gandhi dominated the government. Sceptics, however, doubt if Modi can sustain this approach at a moment when Delhi is a very different place than the one ruled by the Gandhis. The BJP is a more loosely configured party than the Congress, and it might not be easy for Modi to establish an uncontested authority over the party and the government. There is much grumbling across the political class about excessive centralisation of power under Modi and his aloof leadership. There is deep resentment within the BJP, the allied parties and the cabinet at the apparent lack of consultation with senior colleagues. Finding that balance between providing strong leadership and the need for a collegial functioning is a major challenge for Modi. The PM has also found that a majority in the Lok Sabha is not enough to reclaim the power that the executive had ceded to other institutions like judiciary, regulators and media in the Second Republic.

Put simply, Modi has a long way to go before he can overcome the negative trends of the Second Republic. The first months of the Modi government have also made it clear that the very electoral triumph of Modi and the BJP holds within it the seeds of trouble. By threatening to undermine India's core values, the Hindu extremists prevent the construction of a stable and forward-looking Third Republic that could strengthen India's domestic peace, increase its national prosperity and enhance its power position in the international system. A measure of harmony at home and reasonably high economic growth rates of around 8 per cent are bound to generate new diplomatic opportunities for India. What matters for foreign policy is not simply the steady increase in the relative weight of India in world affairs. The nature of great power relations, shifting regional balances and the evolution of the international system as a whole will have a significant bearing on India's engagement with the world. While some of those developments will impose new constraints, many of them will also provide India significant openings. Minimising the impact of adverse developments and taking advantage of the new opportunities will depend on the performance of the Indian State, its political will and bureaucratic capabilities. For all his problems and constraints, Modi appears to have many more opportunities than his recent predecessors to engineer a structural transformation in India's international relations.

The following chapters examine the foreign policy of Modi as it unfolded in 2014 and early 2015. The columns in Chapter Two look at the nature of Modi's diplomatic inheritance from the UPA government that set the stage for the new prime minister. Chapter Three provides insights into Modi's attempt to strengthen relations with India's smaller neighbours and the new emphasis on promoting South Asian regionalism. Chapters Four and Five deal with Modi's approach to India's two most challenging neighbours, Pakistan and China respectively. Chapter Six examines Modi's surprising embrace of the United States. Chapters Seven and Eight look at the new government's policy towards two important regions of India's extended neighbourhood—Asia and the Indian Ocean. Chapter Nine examines Modi's attempts to promote India's soft power. Each of these chapters begins with a brief review of the context and concludes with an assessment of the progress made. Finally, Chapter Ten offers some concluding reflections on the nature and significance of Modi's foreign policy, especially his effort to make India a leading power on the regional and global stage.

CHAPTER TWO

An Ambivalent Legacy

When it took charge of the nation in the summer of 2004, the UPA government inherited a foreign policy account that was in very good shape. The NDA government, under Atal Bihari Vajpayee, cleared a lot of difficult ground from 1998 to 2004. It ended India's prolonged atomic ambivalence, declared India a nuclear weapon power and initiated efforts to resolve the nation's extended dispute with the global nuclear order. Vajpayee opened the door for a transformation of India's relations with both the United States and China and negotiated sensible approaches to the resolution of the Kashmir question with Pakistan and the boundary dispute with Beijing. The economy was poised for its highest growth rates ever and the world was tripping over itself for cooperation with an India that appeared to be on a path of irreversible rise.

Manmohan Singh, who ran with the baton during his first year in office, found it hard to persuade the Congress leadership and his cabinet colleagues to support bold foreign policy initiatives, especially towards the United States and Pakistan. The columns in this section track the meltdown of UPA's global engagement in the last year of its decade-long tenure and the debate on foreign policy in the run-up to the general elections.

Irresolute on World Stage

UPA's policy paralysis saw Delhi stumble on relations with the United States and Pakistan.

If you compare Dr Manmohan Singh's last trip to America as India's prime minister in late 2013 with the first trip of his predecessor Atal Bihari Vajpayee in 1998, a paradox stares at you. India's economic weight and political standing in the world have risen remarkably over the last decade and a half that separated the two visits. Yet, Singh's diplomacy looked listless while that of Vajpayee radiated energy. Representing India at one of its most difficult moments, Vajpayee thought big and acted boldly to pull India out of a tricky diplomatic corner and alter the terms of its global engagement. Singh, who spoke for a much stronger India, appeared irresolute. In September 1998, Vajpayee arrived at the United Nations in New York to a hostile international audience, thanks to the five nuclear tests he had conducted four months earlier, in May. In response, the UN Security Council passed a resolution condemning the nuclear tests of India and Pakistan (which had followed a couple of weeks later) and demanding that the two countries roll back their nuclear and missile programmes.

Tensions with Pakistan were boiling over and there was a growing international perception that Jammu and Kashmir was the 'world's most dangerous nuclear flashpoint'. Any number of world leaders, from America's Bill Clinton to South Africa's Nelson Mandela, thought a forced mediation between India and Pakistan on Kashmir might be a good idea. The US had imposed a range of nuclear sanctions against India in May 1998 and pressed Europe and Japan to intensify the economic pressure on India. Walking into this minefield, Vajpayee did two important things.

One was to leverage the shock of the nuclear tests to turn the ties with the US on their head. In New York, Vajpayee declared India and the US to be 'natural allies'. After the nuclear defiance of the US, Vajpayee was inviting Washington to a strategic re-imagination of bilateral relations. His thesis offended not just the left and sections of the Congress party, but also important sections of the BJP long reared on a diet of anti-Americanism. Foreign policy pundits were apoplectic at Vajpayee's heresy against the canon of non-alignment. It was Vajpayee's departure from received wisdom that opened the door to US support for ending India's nuclear isolation, American neutrality on Kashmir, expansion of bilateral defence cooperation and Washington's endorsement of a stronger Indian role on the global stage.

As he reordered ties with America, Vajpayee also confronted head-on the more complex relationship with Pakistan at a moment when cross-border terrorism was at its peak. In New York, he sat down with his Pakistani counterpart, Nawaz Sharif, and announced the launch of what was then called 'composite and integrated dialogue' with Islamabad. He broke the long-standing taboo on talking to Pakistan about Kashmir and took the first steps towards expanding people-to-people contact between the two nations, including a decision on starting a bus service between Delhi and Lahore. India's bilateral talks with Pakistan took much of the international heat off the Kashmir question. During the Vajpayee years, there were many twists and turns in India–Pakistan relations, including the Kargil War in the summer of 1999 and the attack on Parliament in December 2001. Yet, he sought to sustain the peace process against all odds, for he recognised that limiting tensions with Pakistan was in India's own interest.

Despite belonging to a different party, Singh eagerly embraced Vajpayee's legacy on the US and Pakistan. He understood that the restructuring of relations with the US and a careful management of those with Pakistan were a critical part of India's advancement on the regional and global stage. He took Vajpayee's atomic engagement with America to its logical conclusion—the integration of India into the global nuclear order. He pursued the dialogue with Pakistan under turbulent conditions, negotiated a framework for the resolution of the Kashmir dispute, came close to signing accords on the Siachen and Sir Creek disputes, and worked out a roadmap for normalising trade relations.

Despite his conviction and commitment to these two relationships, there was no escaping the strange defensiveness that had crept into the UPA government's approach to Washington and Islamabad. The Congress was never too enthusiastic about ties with the US. The risk-averse party was also opposed to any bold initiatives towards Pakistan. As a result, the pace of engagement with the US slowed, and even the simple question of the PM meeting Sharif became contentious. The UPA government had steadily lost the courage of conviction as well as the capacity to inject fresh momentum in the engagements with America and Pakistan. Although Singh was in a much better position with the US and Pakistan than the one his predecessor found himself in, the self-confidence of the Vajpayee era had begun to evaporate.

23 SEPTEMBER 2013

Won by UPA 1, Lost by UPA 2

Delhi's ambassadors must speak truth to power on the reversal in India's international fortunes.

It was a British diplomat, Henry Wotton, who famously said at the dawn of the 17th century that 'an ambassador is an honest gentleman sent to lie abroad for the good of the country'. The evolution of diplomacy over the last four centuries has, of course, made this dictum a lot less insightful. But Wotton remains right about one thing. Ambassadors must be honest men and women who are truthful at home. Promoting the nation's interests abroad is but one part of an ambassador's job. Equally important is the duty to apprise the political masters at home of the developments beyond borders, and the opportunities and dangers they present to the national interest. Above all, an envoy should let the sovereign know how the nation looks from a clinical external perspective.

India's ambassadors are in a better position than most to reflect on the undeniable reversal of India's international fortunes in the second term of the UPA government. Having created unprecedented diplomatic opportunities in the first term, the UPA has managed to squander them in the second. To be fair, not everything that went wrong was under the control of the nation's foreign policy establishment. Although the UPA government's failures on the economic front have been the most damaging, there is enough blame to go around the Delhi durbar. Some of it must be put squarely on the timorous worldview of the ruling Congress party. The rest of it belongs to the PM and his foreign policy advisers.

Any review of the UPA government's foreign policy record in the second term would highlight at least three major debacles. The first was the mishandling of the nuclear liability legislation in 2010 that turned one of India's greatest diplomatic victories in the UPA's first term ending India's prolonged atomic isolation into a disaster. After overturning three and a half decades of international nuclear sanctions against India in the first term, the UPA enacted a piece of self-defeating legislation that prevents the participation of foreign and domestic companies in the long overdue expansion of India's nuclear power generation programme. Even India's worst enemies could not have orchestrated it better than UPA 2.

A second disaster was in the wrecking of rare diplomatic opportunities to transform relations with key neighbours, especially Pakistan and Bangladesh. The Congress's fear of looking weak vis-à-vis Pakistan has made Delhi weaker than ever before in engaging Islamabad. If Delhi missed the big moments to make advances with Pakistan in the first term, it created fresh opportunities in the second only to drop the ball at critical moments. In the second term, the UPA also embarked on a bold effort for a comprehensive overhaul of bilateral relations with Bangladesh, only to back off amidst domestic opposition. Its appeasement of every pressure group at home and the habit of looking at foreign policy through the narrow prism of the Congress party's electoral calculus, so visible in its engagements with Dhaka and Colombo, imposed huge costs on India's foreign policy. No national government can ignore domestic politics in the conduct of foreign policy. In its reluctance to make a strong political case for its foreign policy initiatives and the inability to shepherd key domestic constituencies, the UPA government wasted fleeting moments of diplomatic opportunity in the neighbourhood.

Third is a comprehensive misreading of great power relations and the re-injection of the much-discredited non-aligned ideology back into India's worldview. If the rapid advance in India's relationship with the US was the signal achievement of UPA 1, slowing down that momentum in the second has been the big failure under UPA 2. The Congress leadership was never too comfortable with the extraordinary progress in relations with America and nearly pulled the plug on the historic civil nuclear initiative. It was at Prime Minister Manmohan Singh's insistence that the deal was reluctantly pushed through. But the party has had the last laugh in the second term as Delhi introduced some distance between itself and Washington.

This was justified as a return to the presumed non-aligned roots of India's foreign policy and even as a clever manoeuvre to generate major breakthroughs in the relationship with China. Having traded the bird in the hand for two in the bush, the UPA found it had little leverage with Beijing. A strong relationship with the US was critical for shaping India's geopolitical space by expanding its comprehensive national power and reducing the growing strategic gap with China. The rediscovery of non-aligned rhetoric, meanwhile, has made India marginal to the great global debates of our time. Instead of advancing its bilateral strategic partnerships with all the major powers and emerging as a balancer between the East and West and a bridge between the North and South, Delhi has fallen between many stools in the multilateral arena.

Thanks to the approaching general elections, a debate of sorts is bound to emerge on the nation's foreign policy during the decade-long UPA rule. That intensely political and inevitably acrimonious debate is no substitute for an honest professional one among the nation's top diplomats. As the cream of a permanent bureaucracy raised to conduct India's engagement with the world, the envoys have an obligation to speak truth to power. That might be good therapy for the outgoing sovereign, as well as the incoming one.

5 NOVEMBER 2013

India's Region

Delhi must blame itself for losing ground in the neighbourhood.

One of the five foreign policy guidelines that Prime Minister Manmohan Singh articulated in his last annual address to India's envoys in November 2013 was the importance of re-imagining our region. The PM asked the Indian ambassadors to 'recognise that the Indian subcontinent's shared destiny requires greater regional cooperation and connectivity'. The idea of 'India's shared destiny' with its immediate neighbours has been a consistent theme in the PM's statements over the last decade, which has seen significant expansion of New Delhi's regional engagement at both bilateral and multilateral levels.

This idea has a long lineage in India's foreign policy. Under the first non-Congress government formed in 1977 by the Janata Party, the then foreign minister, Atal Bihari Vajpayee, wanted to break the perception that Indira Gandhi's regional policies were 'hegemonic'. Instead, he wanted to promote 'good neighbourly relations'. It was again a non-Congress leader, Inder Kumar Gujral, who injected the notion of regionalism in India's foreign policy. The 'Gujral Doctrine' sought to end India's endless contestations with neighbours and offered to walk the extra mile in resolving long-standing problems.

The economic reforms initiated by Prime Minister P.V. Narasimha Rao, and his finance minister, Manmohan Singh, in the early 1990s provided the foundation for India's economic regionalism. India and its neighbours, it was becoming clear, cannot effectively globalise their economies while neglecting regional integration. As prime minister, Vajpayee consistently emphasised that India can choose its friends but not its neighbours, and pursued peace with Pakistan and a solution to the boundary dispute with China. Despite making bold moves—for example, negotiating on Kashmir with Pakistan and settling the boundary dispute with Bangladesh—Manmohan Singh has lost the momentum because of the inability of his government to build domestic consensus on an enlightened regionalism.

Analysts have drawn attention to the PM's usage of the term 'the subcontinent' rather than the more recent moniker 'South Asia'. 'The subcontinent' more accurately reflects the region's shared history and enduring identity. In using the term, which has begun to gain some traction in recent years, the PM is referring to another goal central to India's foreign policy—the strategic unity of the subcontinent. All great empires that have flourished in the region—the Mauryan, the Mughal and the British Raj—strove to unite the subcontinent and secure it against external and internal challenges. The Partition and its strategic consequences have severely constrained independent India's attempts to build the strategic unity of the subcontinent. India's past insular economic policies have made it even more difficult by sundering the traditional commercial and physical connectivity within the subcontinent. Restoring the lost connectivity, then, stands out as an important strategic objective of India's foreign policy. Delhi must learn to work with multiple sovereignties in the subcontinent and leverage the logic of globalisation to promote shared prosperity across the region.

As part of its quest for primacy in the subcontinent, India has always opposed great power intervention in the region. Realism, however, suggests India cannot exclude the great power involvement in the subcontinent by mere diktat. Delhi's complaint against external meddling in India's neighbourhood, directed traditionally against the West, is now also aimed at China. As the world's second largest economy, China's profile in the region can only rise. China is the largest trading partner to most countries in the subcontinent, including India. On top of it, China has demonstrated its ability to alter the military balance in the subcontinent by helping Pakistan arm itself with nuclear weapons and missiles. In the coming years, Beijing is also likely to become a major supplier of conventional weapons to most of India's neighbours.

Protesting against the role of great powers in the region is futile. India needs a more purposeful policy to build on its natural geographic advantages in the subcontinent, deepen economic integration, promote regional connectivity, and resolve outstanding bilateral political disputes. If India can't sustain a dialogue with Islamabad, ratify agreements negotiated in good faith with Dhaka, and the PM can't even travel to the Commonwealth Summit in Colombo, Delhi is only making it easier for other powers to intervene in the subcontinent. Delhi has itself to blame if the subcontinent eventually stops being India's region.

8 NOVEMBER 2013

'India at Risk': Security Counsel

BJP leader Jaswant Singh on India's territoriality and national security.

The history of independent India will recognise the contributions of many distinguished ministers of the Union cabinet. But it is difficult to recall many from the post-Nehru generations who have reflected on the great policy issues they confronted in office. Jaswant Singh, who served as the minister for foreign affairs, defence, and finance, and headed the Planning Commission, is clearly an exception. Singh's book, *Defending India*, was published as he joined the cabinet in 1998. As the minister for external affairs, Jaswant Singh brought great dignity to the office, managed many crises and contributed to the transformation of India's foreign policy in the Vajpayee years. During his tenure, he also pushed for long overdue reforms of the country's national security establishment. It is with great anticipation, then, one picks up Singh's latest book, *India at Risk: Mistakes, Misconceptions and Misadventures*. He begins by asking a very big question. Why does India continue to flounder when it comes to national security management? Whether it is coping with terrorism or securing our troubled borders with China and Pakistan, the Delhi durbar continues to have huge problems of management.

Jaswant Singh identifies a number of factors, including the debilitating impact of the Partition that broke up the strategic unity of the subcontinent, the turbulence generated by nation-building, the lack of sensibility to India's territoriality, and the failure to develop a statecraft that can get on top of the many security challenges confronting India. Much of the book is devoted to a critical assessment of the 1947–48 Jammu and Kashmir war, the wars with

China and Pakistan in 1962 and 1965 respectively, and the liberation of Bangladesh. This is not the traditional attack from the opposition on Jawaharlal Nehru and the Congress party for their deemed failures. Singh is more philosophical than polemical in his criticisms of Indian mis-steps in the first decades after Independence. Singh has an incisive chapter on what he calls 'India's destructive decades: the 1970s and 1980s', when the nation was at war with itself in the Punjab, Assam and the North-East. He is at his clinical best in assessing India's unsuccessful military intervention in Sri Lanka in the late 1980s.

The last two chapters are of the greatest interest to readers, for they deal with national security issues that Singh was intimately involved with as a senior minister in the Vajpayee government (1998–2004). After all, this was a period when India ended its prolonged atomic ambivalence, conducted five nuclear tests, declared itself a nuclear weapon power, sought to negotiate on Kashmir with Pakistan, launched military operations to vacate Pakistan's Kargil aggression, explored a boundary settlement with China, and coped with the mounting challenges of terrorism. Singh, however, whets the appetite but stops short of serving the main course. The short chapter on nuclear issues does not walk us through the complex manoeuvre that he and his colleagues in the NDA government undertook to soften the negative international reaction and lay the foundation for India's eventual accommodation with the United States and the global nuclear order.

He does much better in his final chapter where he lays out the story of Vajpayee's bus journey to Lahore, the response to the Kargil surprise, the Kandahar hijacking and the Agra debacle with Gen. Pervez Musharraf. His valuable narrative plugs some of the gaps in what is known about these controversial events and lays bare the many dilemmas that he had to deal with as a decision maker. Given his stature and record, we expect more from Singh. A detached but critical review of the lessons from the national security successes and failures in the Vajpayee years, for example, would have been immensely instructive for the next generation of Indian leaders. Perhaps, Singh is still too close to the events to venture in that direction. Despite that limitation, *India at Risk*, elegantly written and well produced, is a rewarding read for anyone interested in India's enduring security challenges.

One would urge Singh to take up on this unfinished task, especially the one tantalising proposition that he begins and ends *India at Risk* with. Singh insists that India will remain 'immobilised in thought' and 'physically impaired in its responses' if it does not break out of the strategic confinement imposed by four lines: the Durand Line, the McMahon Line, the Line of Control, and the Line of Actual Control. Few have thought more deeply than Singh on the imperatives of consolidating India's territoriality. The Congress government, despite a decade-long tenure, has failed to finish what Vajpayee started with Pakistan, China and the neighbourhood. One hopes that in his next book, Singh will elaborate on how India can overcome the consequences of Partition, settle its border disputes, re-imagine its frontiers and restore the strategic unity of the subcontinent.

16 NOVEMBER 2013

Degrees of Irresponsibility

The dangers of playing politics with foreign policy.

The Aam Aadmi Party's controversial foray into Kashmir affairs and the BJP's continuing attacks on UPA government's foreign policy in early 2014 do not bode well for India's national security at a critical moment in domestic politics and great uncertainty in the international environment. The call for a referendum in Kashmir on the presence of the army there by Prashant Bhushan, a senior leader of the AAP, shows how unready the party is for the big stage. The problem is not that Bhushan often has his foot in mouth. After all this is not the first time he has stirred up a controversy on Kashmir. Back in 2011 he had reportedly suggested that a plebiscite should decide whether Kashmir should be part of India. The worry is about the party's facile understanding of national security challenges in Kashmir.

The army has been deployed in Kashmir since the end of the 1980s for a specific reason—to cope with the extraordinary threat to the nation's territorial integrity accentuated by cross-border terrorism aided by the Pakistan army. The AAP seems to forget that Jammu and Kashmir's accession to the Union of India is contested by Pakistan and parts of this frontier state are under the occupation of Pakistan and China. Yet, it is not out of place for a political party to raise questions about the nature, disposition and effectiveness of the army's large-scale deployment in Kashmir for nearly quarter of a century. Instead of responsibly initiating what could have been a useful national debate, the AAP has raised a highly sensitive issue in a cavalier manner. As a new political formation that has captured the nation's imagination in a short span of time, the AAP might be excused for its innocence on national security.

The BJP has no such redeeming explanation for its churlish attitude towards national security. Consider, for example, the party's reaction to Manmohan Singh's comments on the foreign policy record of the UPA government at what probably is the prime minister's last press conference at home. The BJP's criticism of the PM's statement that India was in sight of a breakthrough in the relations with Pakistan and its questioning of the terms of the UPA's Kashmir negotiations with Islamabad are breathtaking in their cynicism. It is well known that Vajpayee authorised negotiations with Pakistan on Kashmir, for the first time since 1963, through a back channel immediately after the NDA came to power in 1998. Interlocutors on the Pakistani side have affirmed that these discussions took place on the basis of the so-called 'Chenab formula' that would have involved some territorial concessions.

Veteran journalist Kuldip Nayar reported in his book *Scoop* (published in 2006) that Vajpayee had told him India and Pakistan 'were almost there' in clinching a Kashmir settlement during the 1998–99 period. Pakistan's Kargil betrayal in 1999 and the failed Agra Summit with Musharraf in 2001 did not stop Vajpayee, who understood the utmost importance of regional peace and reconciliation. Vajpayee's persistence eventually bore fruit in January 2004, when he hammered out a balanced framework of bilateral engagement with Pakistan and authorised Kashmir talks in an environment free of terror. The back-channel talks were led by the national security adviser, Brajesh Mishra, and Musharraf's aide Tariq Aziz. After the BJP lost power in 2004, the UPA government chose to build on Vajpayee's initiative. The new national security adviser, J.N. Dixit, took charge of the process and after his untimely death in January 2005, Satinder Lambah took over.

The contours of this negotiation between Lambah and Aziz, which took place from 2005 to 2007, came out in dribs and drabs. Two features of the negotiations under the UPA, however, were widely known in Delhi's corridors. One, unlike the talks in Vajpayee's first term around the Chenab formula, there would be no Indian territorial concessions in Kashmir. Two, the draft agreement did not violate the Constitution of India, the Constitution of Jammu and Kashmir, and the 1994 parliamentary resolution on Kashmir. The BJP's demand that the PM must reveal the terms of this negotiation is indeed hypocritical. As a ruling party in waiting, the BJP should know that if sensitive negotiations are not held in secret, there will be no agreements to sign in public. The Vajpayee government, then, rightly did not make public the framework of its Kashmir talks with Pakistan.

The problem with the current BJP leadership, however, goes much deeper. Whether it was the nuclear deal with the United States or the negotiations with Pakistan and Bangladesh, the BJP in opposition has put tactical considerations above the national interest by trashing initiatives that it had launched with the US and Pakistan when in power. The BJP's cynicism was reflected in its leaders reportedly telling external interlocutors, in sotto voce, that that they would not let the Congress take the credit for the historic initiatives; they would rather claim it themselves after returning to power. The Congress party, however, deserves even a greater share of the blame for the current foreign policy mess. The party's fear of bold strategic initiatives and the PM's reluctance to make the political case for them saw the squandering of rare strategic opportunities that presented themselves to Delhi over the last decade. The Congress party's political pusillanimity and the BJP's endless opportunism are now being compounded by the AAP's anarchism. The Indian political classes, both old and new, are gravely mistaken if they think national security is fair game in the elections and the contest for power at home can be conducted without reference to the world outside. With the Delhi durbar at its weakest in decades and the national parties in a funk, India's ability to deal with externally induced challenges in the run-up to the elections and after is being undermined by an irresponsible domestic discourse.

9 JANUARY 2014

Modi's World

The BJP manifesto's vagueness on foreign policy could be Modi's opportunity.

Foreign policy is rarely central to elections anywhere in the world. It is no surprise, then, that the foreign policy sections in the manifestos put out by the Congress and BJP in the run-up to the 2014 elections seem an afterthought. Both end up with a long laundry list of disparate propositions. Marginal though they are, the manifestos do offer a peep into the dominant worldview of the Congress and the BJP. Both are disappointing in their inability to comprehend the central imperative of India's foreign policy—the extraordinary international interdependence that defines India's contemporary condition. Nearly a quarter of a century after the launch of economic reforms, more than 50 per cent of the Indian economy is tied to imports and exports. India imports 90 per cent of its hydrocarbon requirements and a growing share of its coal consumption from abroad. The welfare and progress of the Indian people have never depended so much on what happens beyond its borders. And as the tenth largest economy, India too matters to the world more than ever before. That is one reason why there is so much global interest in these elections.

Yet, the assumptions guiding the Congress and the BJP are rooted in a different era. The challenge for India is no longer about preventing the world from impinging on its choices, but to using its growing economic and political weight to shape the external environment to its benefit. The foreign policy section of the Congress manifesto is bizarre in its talk about solidarity with 'socialist' countries and reveals the make-believe world of the party's leadership. The BJP manifesto is not up to speed either. Although some of the new ideas outlined by the BJP's prime ministerial candidate, Narendra Modi, over the last few months did find their way in, the manifesto is quite clearly a triumph for the old guard that is so out of touch with the world.

One new theme in the BJP manifesto is the call, articulated often by Modi, to make the states partners in the execution of Indian foreign policy. Coming from the BJP, with its traditional emphasis on centralisation, the emphasis on the role of states is somewhat counter-intuitive. It comes amid mounting concerns in Delhi's foreign policy establishment that the Congress party has weakened the Centre's hand and ceded a veto to the states, especially Tamil Nadu and West Bengal. The Congress reserves its longest paragraph in the foreign policy section to Sri Lanka as a bow to pressures from Tamil Nadu. Rather than attack the Congress for its appeasement of states, Modi wants to make the state chief ministers allies in boosting Indian diplomacy. The proposition holds much promise, but needs to be fleshed out in greater detail.

A second innovation in the BJP manifesto is the idea of crafting a 'web of alliances' to boost India's weight on the global stage. It stands in contrast to Congress's obsession with the traditional conception of non-alignment. To be sure, the BJP seems to share the Congress's aversion to alliances with big powers like the United States. In fact, neither party mentions relations with the US. The Congress talks about improving relations with all major powers and the BJP says Indian foreign policy will not be led by the big powers. But what about alliances with middle powers and smaller states that are seeking greater security cooperation with India? Delhi established treaty-based alliances with its smaller Himalayan neighbours and defence cooperation with middle powers like Indonesia and Egypt in the Nehru years. More recently, India has signed up for strategic partnerships with a number of countries in the extended neighbourhood. The UPA government has talked the talk, but has been afraid to walk the walk. The reluctance of the defence ministry under A.K. Antony has prevented a vigorous pursuit of military diplomacy. The drift in the economic ministries has undermined Delhi's ability to develop significant strategic economic cooperation with India's partners. Building a web of Indian alliances in Africa, Asia and the Indian Ocean is a big idea whose time has come.

A third important element, a strategic conception of the subcontinent, finds some expression in the Congress manifesto, which says deeper economic engagement with the neighbours is 'critical for realising the true potential of the region'. The BJP criticises the Congress for the recent drift in the relations with the neighbours, but offers little more than the assertion that it will 'pursue friendly relations' with all neighbours. The emphasis is on projecting a muscular regional policy: 'where required we will not hesitate from taking strong stand and steps'. But bravado is not a substitute for a comprehensive neighbourhood strategy. One would have assumed that the BJP would highlight the regional dimensions of Modi's domestic focus on economic development. Instead, the BJP has spewed tough rhetoric on illegal migration from Bangladesh, is unwilling to back a transformation in the ties with Dhaka that the Congress pursued but could not finish, and is unable to focus on trans-border connectivity and regional economic integration. The manifesto has only revealed the BJP's lack of a grand strategy for the region. In the end, though, the BJP manifesto is a classic committee document that seeks to say many things to many people. But its vagueness should offer Modi, as the prospective PM, considerable freedom to put his own stamp on India's foreign policy. Unlike Manmohan Singh, who had to yield constantly to the Congress's self-doubt, Modi might have sufficient authority in the BJP to set his own strategic priorities.

9 APRIL 2014

Through most of his intensive campaign during the general elections of 2014, Narendra Modi, the BJP's prime ministerial candidate, chose to stay away from the details of his foreign and security policies. In the end, he stuck to a simple affirmation that he will uphold the essence of Vajpayee's strategic legacy. The fact, however, is that Manmohan Singh's foreign policy was not very different from that of Vajpayee. Whether it was India's nuclear strategy or the Look East policy, the engagement with great powers or an emphasis on the economic integration of the subcontinent, Singh travelled on the path cut by Vajpayee. In the heat of an election campaign, no one was expecting Modi to acknowledge the foreign policy continuity between the UPA and NDA governments. Modi's emphasis on Vajpayee's foreign policy legacy has offered much needed reassurance all around that India will not abandon its traditional nuclear restraint, continue to seek peace with neighbours and promote regional prosperity through the economic integration of the subcontinent. In reclaiming the Vajpayee legacy, Modi is also distancing himself from the political opportunism of the BJP when it sat on the opposition benches since 2004.

CHAPTER THREE

Neighbours First

One of the most distinguishing features of Prime Minister Modi's foreign policy has been the special emphasis on improving relations with the smaller neighbours. On the face of it, this was in tune with the broad proposition, backed by most political parties and recent governments, that India must devote more diplomatic attention to its neighbours. As Modi's predecessors, Rao, Gujral, Vajpayee and Dr Singh, found out, translating that sentiment into effective policy is not easy. The inability of the bureaucratic establishment to think strategically about the neighbourhood, the reluctance of the political class to back bold new initiatives in South Asia and the new power of state leaders to veto national decisions on neighbours severely complicated India's regional diplomacy.

The gap between articulation of a new vision and implementing it became quite acute under the UPA government. Having won a large mandate in the elections, Modi was certainly much better placed than his predecessors in getting India's act together in the subcontinent. But few expected him to move as quickly and boldly as he did. The columns in this chapter track

Modi's moves on the regional front until early 2015. Given their complexity, India's relations with Pakistan and China are dealt with in separate chapters that follow. The focus here is on other neighbours, especially Bangladesh, Nepal and Sri Lanka, and India's imperatives for pursuing vibrant regionalism.

Renewing India's Regionalism

Modi's invitation to leaders of the neighbouring countries to join his swearing-in ceremony sets the stage for a vigorous regional policy.

Modi's determination to pursue a vigorous regional diplomacy—marked by his invitation to the leaders of the subcontinent and Mauritius to join his inauguration—appears to rest on five foundations. For one, Modi has appreciated the much neglected fact that foreign policy begins at the nation's borders. India's traditional diplomatic discourse is obsessed with grand concepts such as non-alignment and the elusive quest for the leadership of the global South. It has been rather easy for the Indian strategic community to forget the critical importance of tending one's own neighbourhood in the subcontinent and the Indian Ocean. Worse still, Delhi has been unwilling to confront and address the reasons for the steady loss of Indian influence in the region over the last many decades. An India that fails to reclaim its primacy in the subcontinent, Modi can now see, can't really make a lasting impression on the world beyond.

Second, Modi has understood the importance of discarding the diplomatic formalism that has bedevilled India's engagement with the region. Consider, for example, Manmohan Singh's legacy on regional diplomacy. In his decade-long tenure as PM, Singh was either unwilling or unable to step across the borders to catch up with the leaders next door. Singh travelled for regional summits once each in Dhaka, Colombo, Thimphu and Malé. He travelled twice to Kabul and once each to Dhaka and Thimphu on bilateral business. By any measure, this is a dismal diplomatic record. Modi, in contrast, is suggesting that contacts with the neighbours should be made a matter of routine rather than treated as exceptional occasions.

Third, at the level of substance, Manmohan Singh had a clear vision that India's destiny is inextricably linked with that of her neighbours. He articulated the case for regional economic integration and took some important initiatives on trade liberalisation and trans-border connectivity. He was also ready to address long-standing issues with neighbouring countries, including the Kashmir question with Pakistan. But the Congress leadership would not let Manmohan Singh travel to Pakistan even once. It caved in to pressures from the West Bengal chief minister, Mamata Banerjee, and compelled Manmohan Singh to pull back on the very consequential agreements with Dhaka. Yielding to pressures from Tamil Nadu, the Congress leadership prevented the PM from travelling to Colombo for the Commonwealth Summit.

If the Congress put narrow electoral considerations above India's national interests in the region, Modi seems ready to uphold the Central government's responsibility to conduct foreign policy. He can easily follow through by clinching the agreements with neighbours that have already been negotiated and are ready for signature. Modi's rejection of the protests from the BJP's allies and others in Chennai against the visit of Sri Lankan president Mahinda Rajapaksa not only underlines India's new resolve but also improves Delhi's negotiating leverage with Colombo on the question of Tamil minority rights in Sri Lanka. Fourth, in inviting the prime minister of Mauritius to the swearing-in ceremony, Modi is acknowledging Delhi's special relationship with the island nation and its Indian diaspora. The new PM is acutely aware of the urgent need to reverse the UPA government's wanton destruction of this relationship at the very moment when Mauritius is re-emerging as the strategic pivot of the western Indian Ocean.

Finally, Modi appears to have recognised that India's ability to deal with great powers like the United States and China will significantly improve only if and when Delhi can reconstitute the geopolitical unity of the subcontinent. For decades, India has complained about US and Chinese strategic partnerships with Pakistan. More recently, India has watched warily as China's political influence rose rapidly in the subcontinent. Instead of whining about external intervention in the subcontinent, Delhi needs a strategy that builds on India's natural geographic advantage, economic complementarity, historic role as the regional security provider and a shared cultural inheritance. If Manmohan Singh talked the talk on restoring India's regional primacy, Modi might have the political will to walk the walk by resolving long-standing political disputes and promoting economic prosperity across the subcontinent.

26 MAY 2014

Addressing Dhaka

Bangladesh is the test case for Modi's proclaimed commitment to transform relations with neighbours.

If Prime Minister Narendra Modi chose Bhutan as his first foreign destination, the external affairs minister, Sushma Swaraj, has opted for Dhaka. In Bangladesh, as elsewhere in the world, expectations are high that Modi will be a more credible interlocutor than his predecessor. Manmohan Singh had the right convictions on what India ought to do with its neighbours, but he did not have the unstinting support of his own party. Nor did Manmohan Singh mobilise public opinion behind his strategic regional initiatives. Nowhere was the gap between diplomatic ambition and political weakness more evident than in the UPA's engagement with Bangladesh. In 2010, Manmohan Singh and Bangladesh prime minister Sheikh Hasina launched a bold effort to reinvent Indo-Bangla relations. Dhaka addressed India's concerns on cross-border terrorism by extending unprecedented security cooperation. Delhi removed most tariff barriers on Bangladeshi exports to India.

Together they negotiated an interim framework to share the Teesta and resolve the long-standing land boundary dispute. On what should have been a day of celebration in Dhaka in September 2011, the chief minister of West Bengal, Mamata Banerjee, was a no-show. Manmohan Singh was reluctant to sign the Teesta waters accord in the face of her opposition. Although he signed the Land Boundary Agreement, he found it hard to push for its ratification in Parliament.

The UPA government badly let down Sheikh Hasina and the Awami League, and reinforced the traditional scepticism in Dhaka that Delhi is not a reliable partner. Optimists in Dhaka believe that the Modi government is capable of finishing what Manmohan Singh started. Dhaka is not unaware of the fact that sections of the BJP had opposed the agreements with Bangladesh. It is also concerned about some of the tough rhetoric from Modi during the election campaign about cracking down on illegal immigration. Modi and Swaraj can address the concerns in Dhaka and of the Indian states bordering Bangladesh only by demonstrating that a strong strategic partnership will produce win-win outcomes for everyone in the eastern subcontinent. To get there, Delhi and Dhaka must recognise that geography has inseparably interlinked their destinies. For Bangladesh, India is virtually the only neighbour with a border of nearly 4,000 km. (Myanmar is the only other country that shares a border, about 270 km long, with Bangladesh). No wonder Dhaka feels 'India-locked'. For India's north-eastern states, the easiest access to either the Indian mainland or the Bay of Bengal is through Bangladesh.

Managing this geographic interdependence has long been the principal strategic challenge for Delhi and Dhaka. It is only recently that both sides have recognised that they need the other to make progress on a whole range of issues, from internal security to water resource management and economic modernisation.

Delhi and Dhaka can deepen bilateral cooperation in the fight against terrorism and extremism in both the countries. The finalisation of the land boundary will not only clean up the territorial mess left by the Partition of the subcontinent in the east, but also help improve the internal security of both countries. If Delhi must focus on trade facilitation by improving the pitiful infrastructure on the border, Dhaka must begin to see itself as the transit hub between different parts of India. If Dhaka must recognise the benefits of offering overland transit to India, Delhi must contribute to the modernisation of roads, railways and waterways within Bangladesh and coastal shipping in the Bay of Bengal.

If economic integration is now a shared goal for Delhi and Dhaka, they must make it easier for businessmen and tourists to travel across the border. On the important question of illegal migration, the two sides must learn to manage the natural labour mobility in the subcontinent through 'work permits', rather than trying to prevent it unilaterally or denying its existence. Above all, Swaraj should recognise that Delhi's obsession with Pakistan makes it blind to the huge possibilities with Bangladesh. If Pakistan is a problem that India must manage, Bangladesh offers a rare strategic opportunity to transform the geopolitics of the subcontinent. A comprehensive partnership with Dhaka might be the key that will eventually open the door to a productive engagement with Pakistan.

24 JUNE 2014

Drawing Lines in the Water

The resolution of maritime territorial disputes opens the door for stronger regionalism in the Bay of Bengal.

The acceptance by Delhi and Dhaka of an international tribunal's award on the maritime territorial dispute between India and Bangladesh sets the stage for substantive regional maritime cooperation in the Bay of Bengal. India and Bangladesh, in partnership with Myanmar, are now in a position to take the destiny of Bay of Bengal into their own hands at a time when the strategic significance of its waters is drawing the attention of great powers. The judgement pronounced in July 2014 by the Permanent Court of Arbitration in The Hague brings to a close one of the subcontinent's long-festering territorial disputes. The Partition of the subcontinent and China's entry into Tibet in the middle of the last century left India with multiple territorial disputes on its land frontiers. Nearly seven decades later, India's land borders with Pakistan, China, Bangladesh and Nepal remain to be settled. India's record on the maritime front has been a little better. Over the years, India has delimited its maritime boundaries with the Maldives, Sri Lanka, Burma, Thailand and Indonesia. The Hague verdict of July 2014 settles the maritime boundary with Bangladesh. That leaves the maritime boundary with Pakistan the only one to be sorted out.

It is tempting for many in both Delhi and Dhaka to define the verdict in terms of what each side has 'won' and 'lost'. The subcontinent has the tragic tradition of ignoring the opportunity costs of letting boundary disputes simmer and refusing to find reasonable settlements and move on. The inability of India and Bangladesh to settle the dispute all these years bilaterally has prevented the fisherfolk of both countries from effectively exploiting the large but disputed waters of the Bay of Bengal. National companies and their international partners could not drill for oil in the bay that has seen the discovery of many new fields in the last few years.

Given the complexity of the issues involved in such cases, there was never going to be a 'winner takes all' outcome. As in any arbitration, each side won some, but not all, of their arguments at The Hague. Delhi and Dhaka rightly welcomed the verdict of the tribunal as beneficial for the people of both countries. This break from the 'lose-lose' politics of the past reflects the new spirit of friendship between the two countries. The long overdue settlement of the boundary dispute at The Hague underlines the enduring value of international arbitration in settling bilateral disputes, especially those that do not raise existential national security questions. India has accepted such international involvement in the drafting of the Indus Waters Treaty in 1960 and in resolving some of the issues arising from its implementation since then. India also agreed to settle the dispute over the Rann of Kutch with Pakistan through arbitration.

The resolution of the maritime dispute between Delhi and Dhaka in accordance with international law follows a similar settlement between Bangladesh and Myanmar two years ago. This stands in contrast to the escalating maritime territorial disputes in the South China Sea adjoining the Bay of Bengal. China has refused to abide by the principles of international law and has begun to use force to assert its expansive claims over the South China Sea. The settlement of Dhaka's maritime territorial disputes with Myanmar and India now opens the door for substantive regional cooperation in the Bay of Bengal littoral. This cooperation is no longer a luxury but a vital strategic necessity. For the Bay of Bengal is no longer a backwater of the Indian Ocean.

The rise of China and its growing maritime interests in the Indian Ocean have made the Bay of Bengal a theatre of critical interest for Beijing. China's vital sea lines of communication pass through the Bay of Bengal. It is also the closest body of water for many of China's landlocked south-western provinces. China, therefore, is building transport corridors, energy pipelines and new ports in the Bay of Bengal. To cap it all, China is now promoting the idea of a maritime silk road in the Bay of Bengal that connects the Indian and Pacific oceans. Only the very bold will claim that all these developments pose no long-term challenges for India. While Beijing's initiatives do create the possibilities for economic cooperation, Delhi can't afford to ignore the strategic consequences of China's rise for the Bay of Bengal.

A century ago, at the beginning of the First World War, a rising Germany shocked the government of India by having its warship, *Emden*, sneak up to Madras and bombard the city. Three decades later, in the Second World War, Delhi was surprised again by the swift Japanese occupation of the Andaman and Nicobar Islands. As Beijing eyes a vigorous strategic presence in the Bay of Bengal littoral, the Americans can't be far behind and are seeking active maritime collaboration with Bangladesh and Myanmar. India has two choices as its quiescent maritime frontiers to the east come alive. Delhi could keep quibbling with its neighbours on minor territorial issues and allow outside powers to play a larger role in the Bay of Bengal and its vast hinterland. Alternatively, it could quickly implement the boundary settlement with Dhaka, boost trilateral maritime cooperation with Bangladesh and Myanmar, and improve the region's leverage with the external powers.

In the southern Indian Ocean, Delhi has already embarked on trilateral maritime cooperation with the Maldives and Sri Lanka. It is likely to be expanded to include Mauritius and the Seychelles. A similar framework for security engagement with Bangladesh and Myanmar should be at the top of Delhi's agenda in the Bay of Bengal. Beyond that, there are unlimited possibilities for strengthening maritime cooperation with Bangladesh and Myanmar—ranging from joint scientific research to environmental monitoring and from major trans-border projects to trilateral naval exercises. If Delhi decides to play for small stakes in the Bay of Bengal, it will deal itself out of the emerging great game in the east.

14 JULY 2014

Bangla Boundary: Biting the Bullet

Constructing a border of cooperation with Bangladesh should liberate India from one of the major geopolitical constraints imposed on it by the Partition.

In telling the BJP workers in Assam at the end of 2014 that India will go ahead with the ratification of the land boundary agreement with Bangladesh, Prime Minister Narendra Modi has put the imperatives of national interest above the regional populism of his own party. The land boundary agreement signed in Dhaka by Prime Minister Manmohan Singh in September 2011 involves rationalisation of the messy boundary that India inherited from the Partition of the subcontinent. Since it involves the 'exchange' of territories, the agreement's implementation needed a constitutional amendment. The 119th amendment bill was placed in the Rajya Sabha at the end of 2013 amidst vociferous opposition from the Trinamool Congress of Bengal and the Asom Gana Parishad in Assam. While the national leadership of the BJP did not oppose the tabling of the bill, it signalled ambivalence given the opposition from the party unit in Assam.

Much of the debate in Bengal and Assam about the agreement is ill-informed. The agreement deals with tiny enclaves owned by one country but left inside the territory of the other at the time of Partition. This led to the tragedy of many people being left State-less and unable to access the benefits of development from either State. These enclaves have also become major sources of criminal activity. Delhi and Dhaka rightly decided to exchange these enclaves after a survey of opinion in these enclaves—India would 'cede' 111 enclaves amounting to about 17,160 acres and 'gain' 57 enclaves spread over 7,110 acres from the other. The loss and gain of territory here is entirely notional for neither side was in control of these enclaves that they owned in theory since 1947. The overwhelming sentiment among people trapped in these enclaves is to stay put where they are rather than move to the other country.

While the Congress government in Assam supported the agreement, the Trinamool, AGP and the BJP played political football by raising concerns about 'loss' of territory. Modi affirmed that the territorial swap with Bangladesh is in the interests of the nation. He also promised the people of Assam that Delhi will address their concerns on illegal immigration from Bangladesh. By framing an argument that limits the tension between 'national' and 'regional' interests, Modi has set the stage for Parliament's approval of the 119th constitution amendment bill. The standing committee on external affairs had cleared the bill and the Modi government must now move expeditiously to seek approval of the two houses. India's ratification of this agreement will mark a comprehensive territorial settlement of its longest land border. At 4,060 km, India's boundary with Bangladesh is longer than those with China and Pakistan.

Having a settled boundary will now allow Delhi and Dhaka to consider effective management of the border—through more intensive cooperation on countering terrorism and extremism, facilitating trade across this long frontier, building trans-border industrial corridors and preventing illegal movement of people. Constructing a border of cooperation with Bangladesh should liberate India from one of the major geopolitical constraints imposed on it by the partition of Bengal.

1 DECEMBER 2014

Political Pilgrim: Modi in Kathmandu

Modi's celebration of the shared spiritual heritage with Nepal can be combined with a development strategy that can benefit the people of both nations.

Prime Minister Narendra Modi's two-day visit to Nepal in August 2014 drew special political attention to the profound religious intimacy between India and the world's only other nation with a majority of Hindus. There are many countries, with different religious denominations, with which India celebrates shared history, culture and civilisation. But the spiritual affinity between the people of India and Nepal is intense and lived every day. Yet religion has not been of policy consequence in the diplomatic engagement between Delhi and Kathmandu. Until now. A number of new factors make religion quite relevant to the current discourse on India–Nepal relations. Most Indian leaders travelling to Kathmandu do make it a point to visit the Pashupatinath temple. But Modi's prayers at the temple have a special resonance, given the overt religiosity of the prime minister.

When he returned to Varanasi after being elected prime minister, Modi offered prayers at the Vishwanath temple and joined the 'Ganga aarti' at Dashashwamedh Ghat. During her visit to Dhaka last month, External Affairs Minister Sushma Swaraj went to pray at the Dhakeshwari temple. It is no secret that the dates for Modi's visit were finalised with the awareness that visiting Pashupatinath on a Monday of the lunar month, Shravan, is considered especially auspicious.

For most leaders from Pakistan and Bangladesh, an official visit to India would be incomplete without a pilgrimage to Ajmer Sharif. For leaders from Myanmar, Sri Lanka and many other nations in Asia, visiting Bodh Gaya would be an important part of their itinerary. Indian godmen, of course, have long attracted visiting heads of government and state from around the world.

Nepalese leaders across the political spectrum think it is entirely appropriate that Modi visit the Pashupatinath shrine. For Delhi, the policy issue is not about Modi visiting temples in Nepal. The potential danger is about India crossing the line between celebrating the shared religious heritage and blundering into Nepal's domestic debate on the role of Hinduism in the construction of the post-monarchical state. At the turn of the 1960s, King Mahendra declared Nepal a Hindu state and used religion to legitimise the monarchy's power. In 2008, the constituent assembly abolished the monarchy and declared Nepal a democratic, secular and federal republic. Gyanendra, the ousted monarch, and his royalist supporters are hoping that the BJP's ascent to power in Delhi might bring about a change in India's approach to Nepal. Their hopes have been boosted by the RSS-affiliated groups in Nepal that support the notion of a 'Hindu Rashtra'.

Given the deep unpopularity of the monarchy and the perceived link between monarchy and the Hindu state, Modi must unambiguously put down all royalist efforts at claiming a 'special relationship' with the BJP government in Delhi. To avoid any misperception, Modi is well advised to clearly support the current draft constitution's identification of Nepal as a 'federal, secular democratic republic'. Once he steps away from the minefield of Nepal's domestic discourse on the Hindu state, Modi will find the shared Hindu and Buddhist heritage a solid foundation on which to build a new and lasting edifice of bilateral cooperation. As an MP from Varanasi, Modi should highlight the enduring links between Pashupatinath and Kashi Vishwanath. There are multiple other religious connections between the holy shrines of India and Nepal: Lumbini and Bodh Gaya, Janakpur and Ayodhya, Guhyeshwari and Kamakhya, to name a few.

In publicly highlighting these spiritual bonds, Modi touches millions of Nepalese hearts. He should also acknowledge Nepal's historic contribution to the development of two great religions and in preserving many of their traditions over the last two and a half millennia. While the Nepalese are proud of their religious heritage, they are also thirsting for economic development. Modi is in a happy situation where he can combine the celebration of the shared spiritual heritage with a development strategy that can benefit the people of both nations.

For example, the modernisation of the Buddhist circuit in India can be combined with the development of Lumbini and other holy places in Nepal. Similarly, pilgrimage networks centred on Ayodhya and Janakpur can be brought up to world standards. Connectivity has long been a buzzword in India's regional diplomacy. In the case of India's frontier with Nepal, a serious pursuit of connectivity could be simply transformative. Improving connectivity, modernising infrastructure, preserving cultural heritage and promoting tourism are central to Modi's economic programme at home. They are also at the heart of all of Kathmandu's plans to accelerate Nepal's economic growth. The East Asian countries have always been interested in developing and promoting religious tourism in India and Nepal. The growing middle classes in China and India are crying out for better facilities at the priceless holy sites on the Gangetic plains. If Delhi and Kathmandu can get their act together, millions of pilgrims from around the world will pour into the Hindu and Buddhist holy lands and help promote the development of one of the world's poorest regions.

2 AUGUST 2014

Rethinking the Nepal Treaty

Whether Kathmandu wants it or not, it is in Delhi's interest to revise the 1950 Friendship Treaty with Nepal.

The intensity of the relationship between the people of Nepal and India, Prime Minister Narendra Modi suggested in his speech to the Constituent Assembly in Kathmandu in August 2014, can't be measured by 'pieces of paper' signed by the governments of the two countries. The PM's reference to 'pieces of paper' was not rhetorical. It referred to the 1950 'India-Nepal Treaty of Peace and Friendship' between the two governments, which is supposed to codify the special relationship between the two countries. The treaty is the successor to a series of agreements negotiated between the British Raj and the Kingdom of Nepal through the 19th and early 20th centuries. The Nepalese elite sees the treaty as unequal and the symbol of Indian 'hegemony' over Nepal. New Delhi, on the other hand, points to the unique benefits that Nepalese people enjoy in India, including national treatment, an open border and vast employment opportunities. Delhi also points to the fact that all provisions that favour India in the treaty have long gone into disuse; and that the treaty's inequalities are all in favour of Nepal.

Recognising, however, that the treaty had become a lightning rod for anti-India sentiment in Nepal, the Atal Bihari Vajpayee government agreed, nearly a decade and a half ago, to jointly review its provisions with Kathmandu. Delhi has since complained that Nepal's leaders publicly raise the demand for a treaty review, but do not come up with any specific suggestions on how. Put simply, the treaty has become a device for Nepal's leaders to posture against

India, without ever taking the responsibility to suggest its revision. The PM has taken the treaty bull by the horns. He reportedly told Nepal's prime minister, Sushil Koirala, 'You can do exactly what you want with this treaty. You can remove it, you can change it. Come up with a proposal and I will accept it.' Reports also suggest that Modi was eager to have a new treaty in place before the end of his five-year tenure as PM in 2019. In his address to Nepalese leaders at the banquet given by Koirala, Modi urged them not to make the treaty a political issue and invited them to bring forward ideas to recast it. The joint statement issued at the end of Modi's visit said, 'The two prime ministers agreed to review, adjust and update the Treaty of Peace and Friendship of 1950.' The two sides also agreed that 'the revised treaty should better reflect the current realities and aim to further consolidate and expand the multifaceted and deep-rooted relationships in a forward-looking manner'. That the ball is in Nepal's court was confirmed by the joint statement, which said that Kathmandu has 'agreed to provide at the earliest' specific proposals on revising the treaty.

Former French president Charles de Gaulle had famously said that 'treaties, you see, are like roses ... they last while they last'. Covenants and other formal agreements between nations are the product of a specific historical circumstance. When the context, domestic and external, that produced the pact changes significantly over a period of time, there will be little incentive to abide by its terms. Whether Kathmandu wants it or not, it is in Delhi's interest to revise the treaty with Nepal. Delhi certainly needs a new compact with Kathmandu that has strong political support in Nepal and provides a sensible basis for mutually beneficial engagement in the new 21st century. The 1950 treaty was concluded at the request of Nepal, whose rulers were frightened by communist China's advance into Tibet. India, as the successor to the Raj and its legacy of protecting small states in the subcontinent and beyond, stepped in to support Kathmandu. Nepal has long stopped seeing China as a threat and many aspects of the bilateral security cooperation have lapsed. Nepal is now a democracy and its leaders are acutely conscious of national sovereignty. As it waits for specific proposals from Kathmandu, Delhi on its own must imagine and debate the contours of a new strategic partnership agreement with Nepal that is rooted in the principle of sovereign equality and deepens security and economic cooperation between the two countries on a pragmatic basis.

6 AUGUST 2014

India's Lanka Opportunity

After the defeat of Rajapaksa, India has a chance to revive its ties to Lanka.

As a new government led by Maithripala Sirisena takes charge in Sri Lanka after the presidential elections in January 2015, India has a valuable opportunity to arrest the unfortunate drift in bilateral relations over the last few years. The government of Narendra Modi, less constrained internally than the UPA government, is in a good position to rebuild the partnership with a country that occupies a vital position on India's maritime frontiers to the south. The reluctance of the outgoing president, Mahinda Rajapaksa, to address India's concerns on much needed political reconciliation with the Tamil minority after the 2009 victory over the Liberation Tigers of Tamil

Eeelam in the civil war in Sri Lanka that began in the early 1980s was a major source of tension between Delhi and Colombo.

India also watched warily Rajapaksa's growing political warmth towards China. Beijing's growing presence in the Sri Lankan economy, especially its involvement in the development of strategic infrastructure like the Hambantota port and the frequent appearance of Chinese naval ships at the Colombo port had generated considerable anxiety in Delhi's national security establishment.

Rajapaksa's active support to the Chinese proposal on the maritime silk road during the visit of President Xi Jinping to Colombo in September 2014 had magnified Delhi's concerns about Colombo's embrace of Beijing.

The UPA government, which was supportive of Rajapaksa's war against the LTTE terror, steadily lost much goodwill in Colombo amidst the vacillations in its Lanka policy under pressure from Tamil Nadu. Delhi's flip flops at Geneva in the United Nations debates on the human rights situation in Lanka were compounded by Prime Minister Manmohan Singh's decision, under pressure from the Congress leadership, to skip visiting Colombo for the Commonwealth Summit in November 2013. If the UPA government was accused of ceding a veto to Tamil Nadu over the country's foreign policy towards Lanka, Modi sought to restore some flexibility to Indian diplomacy by inviting Rajapaksa to his swearing-in ceremony last May in spite of the objections of then Chief Minister J. Jayalalithaa. With a solid majority of its own in the Lok Sabha the Modi government must now find a better balance between India's interest in securing Tamil minority rights in Sri Lanka and the broader imperative of developing a stronger strategic partnership with Colombo. Although Sirisena has won strong backing from the Tamil minority in the election, he may not necessarily find it easy to address India's concerns given his need to maintain support from the majority Sinhala community. India, then, will have to move with considerable political finesse in taking up the Tamil question afresh with the new government. Delhi can't be seen as either abandoning the issue or trying to impose its will on Colombo.

Dealing with Colombo's China relationship might be equally tricky. Rajapaksa's dealings, economic and political, with China have become controversial within Sri Lanka, and Sirisena has promised to evolve a more balanced approach in its relations with Beijing and Delhi. India, however, might be unwise to expect that Colombo will simply discard the China relationship that has given a range of new economic and strategic options to Sri Lanka. For the Modi government, the challenge lies in finding ways to deepen its own economic and military cooperation with Sri Lanka and accelerate the implementation of a variety of projects with Colombo. There is no doubt that the issues involved—domestic political order and independent foreign policy—are highly sensitive to a sovereign Sri Lanka. Yet, the arrival of a new government in Colombo and a stronger political dispensation in Delhi last May have created the space to explore the prospect for an accommodation of each other's interests.

10 JANUARY 2015

SAARC: Towards Positive Unilateralism

Modi should act unilaterally to nudge the subcontinent towards integration.

For all its trappings of a multilateral organisation, the South Asian Association for Regional Cooperation is only an aggregation of India's bilateral relations with its neighbours. This is the reason why the subcontinent is eager to see how Prime Minister Narendra Modi approaches SAARC. The PM had raised expectations that India will take the leadership of the region by his surprise invitation to all the SAARC leaders to attend his swearing-in ceremony. His visits to Bhutan and Nepal have reinforced those hopes. Modi, however, has a problem. He has inherited a dysfunctional SAARC, whose failures are rooted in geography and history. As the largest country located at the heart of the subcontinent, India has borders with all its neighbours. Only two other members, Pakistan and Afghanistan, have a border with each other. It is no big surprise then that most of the regional trade is actually bilateral trade between India and its neighbours. So are the problems that come from a common border. That takes us to the history of these frontiers. The Partition of the subcontinent created new borders and territorial disputes within it. Nearly seven decades later, India does not have settled borders with either Pakistan or Bangladesh. In the north-west, Kabul does not accept Islamabad's claims that the Durand Line drawn by the British Raj between undivided India and the subcontinent at the end of the 19th century is the legitimate boundary between Afghanistan and Pakistan.

Territorial disputes would not have mattered if India and its neighbours had built open economies. Instead they all turned to state socialism that de-emphasised trade and connectivity. As a consequence, what was an integrated economic space under the Raj broke up into several inward-oriented markets. The global compulsions for economic reform in the early 1990s had also set the stage for regional integration. If Delhi has been a hesitant reformer at home, it has been equally tentative in the efforts to rewrite the economic map of the region. The few initiatives that India has taken in SAARC in recent years have, however, run into political problems. For example, Pakistan appears reluctant to sign the regional agreements on rail, road and energy connectivity that have been negotiated. Even if it signs them, it is by no means guaranteed that Islamabad will implement them. The experience of the South Asian Free Trade Agreement (SAFTA) that Pakistan was unwilling to extend to India is a case in point. Pakistan's argument is simple: as long as it has political problems with India, it will not let regional economic integration proceed.

The merits of this argument are for the Pakistanis to decide. Whether Delhi agrees with the Pakistani argument or not it must come to terms with it. Where does that leave the PM, who has talked ambitiously about trade and connectivity for the subcontinent? Modi has three options. One is to focus on a two-speed SAARC. As Delhi waits for better relations with Pakistan, it could move in the interim towards sub-regional cooperation. In the east, India can take steps to foster integration with Nepal, Bhutan and Bangladesh. In the south, it can construct deeper links with the Maldives and Sri Lanka. Second is to build on trans-regional institutions like the Bay of Bengal Initiative which connects the eastern subcontinent with parts of South-East Asia or join China's silk road initiatives that hope to connect different parts of the subcontinent with various regions of China.

While India can do much on the first and second, it is the third way that offers Modi the greatest opportunity—unilateral action. Modi, for example, has already proposed, unilaterally, to build a SAARC satellite for use by its neighbours. He could open the Indian market for goods produced in the neighbouring countries by reducing tariff and non-tariff barriers and improving trade facilitation. Delhi could also consider transit to its neighbours—for example, letting overland trade between Bangladesh on the one hand and Nepal and Bhutan on the other. Modi can also announce unilateral visa liberalisation. He could also unveil an Indian financial facility for liberal lending to trans-border connectivity projects in the subcontinent. If he can break from Delhi's old mindset, a strategy of positive unilateralism would allow Modi to push the subcontinent a little faster towards long overdue regional integration.

26 NOVEMBER 2014

If the subcontinent has been waiting long for India's leadership in promoting regional integration, Modi has begun to take the initiative. He has ended the prolonged political neglect of the neighbours and has demonstrated the ability to connect to the governments and people of the region. At the SAARC summit in Kathmandu, and in his bilateral visits to Bhutan, Nepal and Sri Lanka, Modi has signalled the willingness to take unilateral steps to promote regional integration and work with sub-regional cooperation where possible.

Yet, Modi has much work to do. Translating his regional vision into practical steps requires sustained pressure on the

Indian establishment to rethink the manner in which it deals with the neighbours. Modi understands the logic of opening India's growing market to its neighbours and moving forward quickly on connectivity within and across India's frontiers and improving trade facilitation. While India's aid volumes in the subcontinent have significantly increased in recent years, its ability to implement projects in time remains problematic. India's ability to resolve long-standing problems with the neighbours is complicated by the fact that Delhi looms large in their domestic politics. Finding a balance between encouraging the neighbours to move in the right direction and complicating the internal dynamics of these nations through heavy-handed intervention will be a political art that Modi will have to master. As other major powers, especially China, deepen their ties with its neighbours in the subcontinent, Delhi can't keep them out by a mere fiat. Modi needs a policy that will maximise India's own advantages of geography, history and culture.

CHAPTER FOUR

The Pakistan Problem

Dealing with the Pakistan that emerged out of the ashes of the Cold War has been the most important challenge for Delhi since the late 1980s. Islamabad's successful acquisition of nuclear weapons neutralised Delhi's conventional superiority and ended the tilt in the regional balance towards India after the vivisection of Pakistan in 1971. The Pakistan army, buoyed by the use of jihad against the Soviet Union in Afghanistan, unveiled a similar strategy against India from the late 1980s. Governments of various hues that ruled Delhi since then tried hard for a political reconciliation with Pakistan, but with little success.

BJP's Atal Bihari Vajpayee, after much trial and error, worked out a framework for normalisation of bilateral relations, but the clock ran out on him. His successor Manmohan Singh, who had all the time, came close to a settlement of the Kashmir issue with Pakistan, but did not have the political backing in the Congress party to formalise the agreement. Narendra Modi, who relentlessly bashed Pakistan when he was the chief minister of Gujarat, tempered his rhetoric in the 2014 elections, and surprised the world by his outreach to the Pakistan prime minister, Nawaz Sharif, after the elections. The resurgence of tensions on the border and Islamabad's engagement with the Kashmiri separatists saw Modi suspend the talks with Pakistan in August 2014. Recognising the problems continued disengagement would create for India, Modi lifted the suspension of political contacts in February 2015. But he is some distance away from crafting a coherent strategy towards Pakistan. The following columns track Modi's roller-coaster ride on Pakistan.

Creating Space on Pakistan

It would be unwise to assess Modi's approach to Pakistan by using the traditional metrics of India's domestic political discourse.

The BJP election manifesto released in April 2014 has left some room for its prime ministerial candidate Narendra Modi in the conduct of India's relations with Pakistan—one of the most challenging accounts of the nation's foreign policy. By avoiding inflammatory rhetoric on Pakistan in the manifesto, the BJP has sought to dampen the speculation around the world that Modi's leadership of India will lead to an inevitable confrontation with Pakistan. Prime Minister Manmohan Singh's diplomacy towards Pakistan in the second term of the UPA was weighed down by the terror attack on Mumbai at the end of November 2008. Over the last few years, he struggled to strike a balance between the need to get the plotters of the attack to justice and the unavoidable imperative of engaging Pakistan. The

Congress party's manifesto highlighted this dilemma by stating that it will 'calibrate the dialogue' with Islamabad to the 'delivery on accountability for 26/11 as well as dismantling of the infrastructure of terrorism on Pakistani soil'.

The BJP certainly refers to the increasing terror attacks in India by 'Pakistan-backed terror groups' and affirms 'zero tolerance towards terrorism'. At the same time, it asserts that India 'will pursue friendly relations' in the neighbourhood. It also insists that 'where required we will not hesitate from taking strong stand and steps', without elaborating on what they might be. The BJP also argues that peace in the region 'is essential for South Asia's growth and development'. It accuses the UPA of presiding over a drift in India's relations with the neighbours. This broad framework, of course, lets Modi, if he indeed becomes the next prime minister, to make a fresh start with Pakistan on the nature and terms of a future dialogue. That, of course, has never been easy, especially when it comes to the connection between cross-border terrorism and dialogue with Pakistan.

7 APRIL 2014

Pakistan in Modi's Eyes

The Pakistan policy will define Modi's room for manoeuvre at home and abroad.

Amidst mounting regional and international concerns about India's relations with Pakistan under a BJP-led government, Modi has sought to calm those fears in the run-up to the election in May 2014. Modi suggested that there would be no radical departures in India's foreign policy, especially towards Pakistan, under a government led by him. He underlined, instead, the importance of engaging Pakistan and insisted that 'anger' can't be the basis for a policy towards our western neighbour. He also appears to have understood the need to address the widespread international concern that a government led by him might abandon India's traditional nuclear restraint and adopt the more risky approaches. If the BJP manifesto talked about revising the nuclear doctrine, Modi made it absolutely clear there was no question of changing India's policy on the no-first-use of atomic weapons.

The government in Pakistan, like most others, has no problem in recognising that the BJP's rhetoric during elections is not necessarily a reflection of the party's policies when in government. Islamabad is putting out signals that it is eager to open a dialogue with the next government and is ready for formal political contact with it at the earliest. The deeply polarised Indian debate on secularism and the controversy over Modi's role in the 2002 Gujarat riots have, however, reinforced fears in Pakistan about a BJP victory in these elections. The lower the political debate in India sinks, the greater the political discomfort in Pakistan will be with a Modi-led government.

At the same time, there is some hope in Pakistan that a strong leader like Modi might be better equipped than Prime Minister Manmohan Singh to move the bilateral relationship forward. Pakistani leaders across the political spectrum and in the military have been deeply disappointed with the UPA government, which repeatedly raised expectations of a big breakthrough in bilateral relations over the last decade but did not have the political courage to follow through.

India's political passions on secularism and communalism make little sense in Pakistan, which is a Muslim-majority State and an

Islamic republic. Pakistan's foreign policy establishment attaches little operational value to secularism in engaging India.

Islamabad remembers that Atal Bihari Vajpayee, representing a 'Hindu nationalist' government, travelled to Pakistan twice. Under far more difficult circumstances, Vajpayee had kept the dialogue going with Pakistan and launched bold initiatives. Pakistan is acutely aware that the 'secular' Congress would not even let Manmohan Singh travel across the border, despite repeated requests from Gen. Pervez Musharraf, former president Asif Ali Zardari and Nawaz Sharif. Nor is it a secret that the champions of secularism in the cabinet, like Arjun Singh and A.K. Antony, were the most vociferous opponents of any reasonable accommodation with Pakistan.

What matters to Islamabad is not the political label attached to Modi but the kind of policies he might pursue if he comes to power. If Modi embarks on a confrontation with the Muslim minority at home and adopts an adventurous policy towards Pakistan, his government would quickly be weakened and become vulnerable to multiple pressures—regional and international. On the other hand, if Modi addresses the genuine fears of the Muslim minority at home and begins an engagement with Pakistan, his room for manoeuvre at home and abroad will significantly improve. Given the unprecedented negative international image Modi has acquired, a sensible and pragmatic approach to Pakistan could bring him extraordinary diplomatic rewards.

22 APRIL 2014

The Pakistan Paradox

Explaining Pakistan's 'geostrategic curse'.

Few countries get the kind of international political and policy attention that Pakistan draws. The nation's pivotal role in shaping the global war on terror and the American occupation of Afghanistan after 9/11 has generated much work from journalists and policy wonks in recent years. T.V. Paul, a reputed scholar of international relations based at McGill University in Canada, joins the effort to understand the political paradox that Pakistan is. Unlike the fleeting reportage and instant analyses, Paul's book, *The Warrior State: Pakistan in the Contemporary World,* digs deep into the causes of State failure in the country. It might be one of the world's poorest countries, but Pakistan has played a significant role in the great power conflicts since the end of World War II. The United States and China have long valued their partnership with the Pakistan army and showered it with valuable assistance for more than half a century.

For the kingdoms of the Gulf, especially Saudi Arabia, the Pakistan army is an integral part of their national security calculus and they have always bailed Pakistan out of financial troubles.

If Pakistan's ISI is considered one of the world's most powerful spy agencies, its diplomats draw much international respect for their sophistication. The not-so-discreet charms of Pakistan's thin ruling elite can bowl over even the most ardent opponents of the nation. Its writers and artists are now making a big mark on the global scene. Despite all these advantages, Pakistan appears to have put itself on the brink of collapse. Pakistan's economy is in a shambles and the army is desperately trying to gain control over its lawless western borderlands that are home to the world's top terrorist organisations.

Violent extremism and sectarian hatred are tearing apart Pakistan's social fabric.

Paul looks at three important ideas to explain the tragedy of Pakistan. One is the concept of 'geostrategic curse'. It is akin to the 'resource curse' which turned out to be the bane of many countries blessed with an abundance of valuable natural resources like oil. Pakistan, which was blessed with extraordinary geopolitical leverage after the Partition of the subcontinent, could not turn it into a tool for national development. Instead, its elites got used to the easy extraction of geopolitical rent, from the major powers as well as the Islamic world, and were unwilling to pursue the hard task of nation-building. Second, Paul argues that after independence, Pakistan developed a worldview that he calls 'hyper-realpolitik' that overstated the dangers of external threats and under-emphasised the imperatives of domestic political and economic development. Third, feeding into this was Pakistan's paranoid quest for strategic parity with India which in turn led to the dominance of the military over the Pakistani State and prevented the emergence of sustainable domestic political institutions and a viable economic strategy.

In themselves, none of these explanations are novel. Paul's success, however, rests in locating the study of Pakistan in the broader context of political development in the post-colonial world. Unlike many of his peers in political science departments, Paul communicates with easy prose, making *The Warrior State* intellectually stimulating without being pedantic. For Paul, the story of Pakistan serves a larger purpose: to examine the various theories on the relationship between war and development. Paul contests the argument, based on European experience, that war-making compels the creation of an efficient and modernising state. Paul argues that 'Pakistan's experience shows that the war-making state may bring neither economic development nor political cohesion. If anything can bring prosperity in the globalised world of the 21st century, it is likely to be a state that reduces the role of military and war-making efforts'. Paul reinforces the point by comparing Pakistan's experience with that of Brazil, Turkey and South Korea, which were once authoritarian states. He argues that all three of them have successfully transformed themselves into 'developmental states', while Pakistan has not. Paul's use of political theory to explain the evolution of Pakistan makes *The Warrior State* a very distinctive contribution to the literature on the contemporary subcontinent.

The book certainly helps the Indian strategic community develop a cold and detached approach to understanding Pakistan and rise above the high emotional quotient that guides Delhi's daily discourse on this difficult neighbour.

To develop a successful policy towards Pakistan over the longer term, however, India must combine Paul's clinical approach with much sensitivity to the modern history of the subcontinent—especially the origins of Partition and its bitter consequences. Even more important, India needs a measure of genuine empathy with the people of Pakistan to leaven Paul's crystal clear judgements on state failure in Pakistan.

21 JUNE 2014

Powerful and Insecure

Is a fundamental change in the Pakistan army's strategic culture possible?

Few armies in the world attract the kind of policy and scholarly attention that the Pakistan army does. Rightly so, for its institutional primacy at home and strategic influence abroad have few parallels. Many armies have run their countries, but most of them had to eventually yield to democratic change and civilian control. The Pakistan army, however, exercises extraordinary power, whether in the barracks or the chancelleries. It controls Pakistan's nuclear arsenal, manipulates its domestic politics, shapes its internal security and runs the critical accounts of the country's foreign policy with India, Afghanistan, China, the Gulf and the United States. Given Pakistan's enduring geopolitical significance since Partition, the army's role there has been consequential not just for the international relations of the region but way beyond. Whether it is the war on terror, the politics of nuclear proliferation, securing the volatile Gulf region, or Great Power rivalries, the Pakistan army pops up as a critical factor in world politics.

For India, the Pakistan army headquartered in Rawalpindi has emerged as the principal stumbling block to the normalisation of relations with its important neighbour to the west. The Pakistan army has never won a conventional war against India, but Rawalpindi has sustained a prolonged low intensity conflict against Delhi by nurturing anti-India terror groups on its soil. It has repeatedly stymied the efforts by civilian leaders in Islamabad to explore even a limited détente with India in pursuit of Pakistan's enlightened self-interest. An appreciation of what makes the Pakistan army tick should, therefore, be of a high priority for Delhi's policy makers and of great interest to Indian civil society. Christine Fair and Aqil Shah have given us two solid works on the Pakistan army that help enrich the Indian and global understanding of its role in shaping Pakistan's domestic politics and external policies.

Fair, a well-known American scholar of the subcontinent, offers powerful insights into the sources of the army's dominance and examines the prospects for a potential change in the coming years. She begins her book, *Fighting to the End: Pakistan Army's Way of War*, by posing a simple puzzle: why does the Pakistan army look like an irrational actor? Why does it promote terrorism against India and Afghanistan even when the consequences destabilise Pakistan itself? What drives the insecurities of the Pakistan army even after it acquired nuclear weapons and blunted India's conventional military superiority? Why can't Rawalpindi accept even a temporary truce with India to secure its more immediate interests at home and beyond?

Fair looks for the answers in the 'strategic culture' of the Pakistan army. By poring over its official publications, examining its self-beliefs and tracking its evolution as an institution, Fair comes to some definitive conclusions that compel all those who have business to do with Pakistan to rethink their assumptions. She argues that the Pakistan army's concerns about India 'are not purely or even mostly security driven'. It is about ideology. The army sees itself protecting not merely the territorial borders of Pakistan but its 'ideological frontiers'. Rawalpindi sees Pakistan locked in a civilisational conflict with India. Fair concludes that 'for the army, resisting India's rise is a necessary condition for the survival of Islamic Pakistan'.

Fair also offers a very important insight into the army's rather unconventional views on victory and defeat in its unending struggle against India. She suggests that the Pakistan army does not view its inability to win multiple wars against India as 'losing'. For Rawalpindi, sustaining the ability to challenge Delhi, and to challenge India's rise, is in itself the prize. If accepting the territorial status quo is a defeat for the Pakistan army, it feels duty-bound to revise it. In its revisionist quest, Fair suggests, the Pakistan army will continue to take significant risks, rather than do nothing. If Fair focuses on the implications of the Pakistan army's doctrine for the region and the world, Shah turns to the equally important role of the army in domestic politics. Like Fair, he too delves deep into the Pakistan army's mindset and its self-perception as the guardian of the nation. In his work, *The Army and Democracy: Military Politics in Pakistan*, Shah asks the old question, 'Who guards the guardians?' He examines the reasons for the evolutionary path taken by the Pakistan army after Partition, which diverges from that of its counterpart in India. He tracks the evolution of the army's views on civil-military relations by focusing on specific historical junctures in Pakistan's history, the moments of transition from civilian to military rule and vice versa.

Shah and Fair offer valuable analyses on the conditions—internal and external—under which the Pakistan army's strategic culture might change. Despite the two civilian governments that have taken power since General Pervez Musharraf stepped down in 2008, Shah is not hopeful that the Pakistan army can really be pushed back into the barracks. He suggests that civilian supremacy could become a 'euphemism for the military's formal and active participation in matters of war and peace' and legitimise the army's 'non-democratic privileges'. If Shah is cautiously pessimistic, Fair insists that India, the US and others 'should abandon their hopes' for a fundamental change in the strategic culture of the Pakistan army. Defining Pakistan as a 'greedy state', Fair suggests any appeasement of the Pakistan army, in the hope of changing its behaviour, would only reinforce its revisionist pursuits. The conclusions of Shah and Fair on the army's unshakeable stranglehold over Pakistan's domestic structures and foreign policies raise basic questions about Delhi's current strategy of engaging Islamabad. If India's problem is not about finding diplomatic accommodation or stabilising military equilibrium, Delhi might have to figure ways to contest Rawalpindi's ideological premises.

19 JULY 2014

No Table for Three

On Kashmir, Modi wants to return to pure bilateralism with Pakistan and will not accept Islamabad's talks with separatists.

Prime Minister Narendra Modi's decision to cancel the foreign secretary-level talks with Pakistan in August 2014 has drawn much political flak at home and generated some international concern that the NDA government might be departing from its proclaimed commitment to improve relations with the neighbours. Although many motivations have been attributed to the decision, the principal rationale is not difficult to discern—to change the terms of the dialogue with Pakistan on the question of Jammu and Kashmir. Delhi's main argument is that Pakistan high commissioner Abdul Basit's meetings with Kashmiri separatist leaders amounted to an unacceptable interference in India's internal affairs.

Pakistan's spokesperson, as well as the NDA government's critics in India, point to the fact that Delhi had chosen to live with the engagement between Islamabad and Kashmiri separatists for many years. They argue that Delhi's decision to cancel the talks is an unfortunate and unexpected departure from the two-decade-old Indian policy. That there is a discontinuity in India's approach is exactly right. The Modi government appears to have come to the political judgement that it will no longer accept the involvement of the All Party Hurriyat Conference, a collection of Kashmiri separatist groups, in the India-Pakistan dialogue. Delhi wants to put the Kashmir question back in a strictly bilateral, inter-governmental framework with Islamabad.

The continuing turbulence in Kashmir, the frequent military crises with Pakistan and the consequent international pressures to engage Islamabad saw India reluctantly yield some space for the Hurriyat in the peace process nearly two decades ago. Since then, Delhi has often directly engaged the Hurriyat, opened back-channel talks with Pakistan on resolving the Kashmir question, allowed contact between the Hurriyat and Islamabad and facilitated the travel of separatists to Pakistan. Throughout this period, both Pakistan and the separatists pressed for a trilateral dialogue. Delhi rejected a table for three but agreed willy-nilly for three separate bilateral tracks. The Modi government is now saying there is no place for the Hurriyat in the peace process with Pakistan. Delhi's new approach is a bold gamble, to say the least. The Modi government's rethinking on Kashmir came into view with its decision to end some of the freebies to the United Nations Military Observer Group in India and Pakistan (UNMOGIP), based in Delhi and J&K since 1949. Although Delhi thinks the UNMOGIP has outlived its utility, it is some distance away from simply asking the UNMOGIP to leave. Clearly, Delhi is keen on ending the vestiges of an international presence in Kashmir.

If Delhi succeeds in getting Pakistan to accept bilateralism on Kashmir, it will be a major political triumph for India. Despite the challenges it confronts at home and on its western frontiers, however, Pakistan is unlikely to return to status quo ante and drop the Hurriyat proxy. The Hurriyat has been a symbol of India's own failures in J&K and of Pakistan's capacity to intervene across the Line of Control. It is one thing for the Modi government to declare that the Hurriyat is beyond the pale. It is entirely another to alter the ground realities in J&K. Equally difficult is the challenge of managing the Kashmir frontier with Pakistan. The ceasefire, which has been in place since the end of 2003, has been fraying for some time. If Pakistan has the ability to raise tensions on the LoC and the International Border in Kashmir, India needs an effective strategy to manage the escalation dynamic. Delhi needs to maintain tight political control over Indian military responses to Pakistani provocations and must avoid drifting into a conflict it does not want. Tough rhetoric is no substitute for calm reflection on how to cope with the multiple consequences of military escalation.

Given the presence of nuclear weapons in the arsenals of India and Pakistan, any escalation of border tensions or a vigorous Indian response across the LoC in the event of a major terror attack will quickly draw the international community into the regional dynamic. Foreign ministers from the West will fly into the subcontinent urging India and Pakistan to stop fighting and start talking.

Any number of busybodies will want to mediate between Delhi and Islamabad on Kashmir. While internationalising the Kashmir question has always been part of Pakistan's strategy, preventing external intervention has been a major Indian political objective. It is India's careful engagement with Pakistan and a dialogue on

Kashmir that have kept the major powers at arm's length. Any serious breakdown of the peace process will bring the great powers back into play and undermine Modi's new emphasis on bilateralism.

As the NDA government recalibrates India's Kashmir and Pakistan policies, Delhi must do a much better job explaining the logic behind the cancellation of the foreign secretary talks, widely seen as abrupt. It must let the international community—especially Pakistan's friends, including the United States, China and Saudi Arabia—know that India is not abandoning the peace process with Islamabad and is ready to deal with all outstanding issues, including the Kashmir question, within a bilateral framework. Above all, Delhi must keep open all channels of communication with Pakistan. The NDA government is betting that the changed circumstances and India's own improved international standing since the 1990s allows it to reframe the dialogue with Pakistan. If Delhi can't get its internal act together in J&K, prevent major terror attacks across the nation and bring synergy between the military management of the border and international diplomacy, Modi's gamble could turn out to be rather risky and politically unsustainable.

21 AUGUST 2014

Modi's Cricket Diplomacy

India should construct a new framework of engagement with Pakistan instead of merely returning to the earlier unproductive dialogue.

Cricket has always come in handy for the leaders of India and Pakistan to signal goodwill towards each other and break the political ice at difficult moments in bilateral relations. So it has for Prime Minister Narendra Modi, who suspended the dialogue with Pakistan in August 2014. Delhi's capricious move at once reversed the bonhomie that Modi had generated with Nawaz Sharif when the Pakistani PM joined other South Asian leaders at the swearing-in ceremony of the new Indian government last May. Whatever the political logic behind the suspension, it had become increasingly counter-productive for the Modi government to be seen as resisting a dialogue with Pakistan. Islamabad has been portraying Modi as intransigent and was mounting pressure on the international community to push Delhi towards a dialogue.

Although US president Barack Obama did not publicly bring up the question of resuming the India-Pakistan dialogue, it is believed the two leaders had talked about the issue during their conversation at the Hyderabad House on the eve of the Republic Day celebrations. On his part, Modi apparently reaffirmed his commitment to the peace process and his readiness to engage Islamabad in a framework that responds to Delhi's concerns on cross-border terrorism, is focused on expansive economic cooperation, and avoids the kind of posturing that Islamabad does on Kashmir. Modi reminded Obama of his quick and empathetic response to the horrible terror attack on a school in Peshawar last December and his deep disappointment at the reports that Pakistan was going to release the main plotter of the 26/11 attacks on Mumbai.

It was not just Obama who was urging Modi to renew the dialogue with Pakistan. Many other international interlocutors including the leaders in the neighbourhood have encouraged Modi not to turn his back on Pakistan. Nor is all the clamour for reviving the dialogue coming from abroad. In his address to the Indian envoys gathered in Delhi for annual confabulations, President Pranab Mukherjee reminded the government of the need to revitalise its regional peace overtures. The opening of the Cricket World Cup in mid-February 2015 thus provided Modi with an opportunity to end the six-month-old diplomatic impasse with Pakistan. He called up Sharif to wish Pakistan well in the World Cup and offered to send the new foreign secretary, S. Jaishankar, to Islamabad.

The PM was careful to present the outreach to Pakistan as part of extending goodwill to all the five South Asian nations participating in the World Cup. Jaishankar's trip to Pakistan is also being billed as part of the foreign secretary's travel to all the capitals of the subcontinent. The attempt to couch the initiative in South Asian terms indeed helps the Modi government to sidestep potential domestic criticism of a 'diplomatic climb-down' on Pakistan. It is important to note that Jaishankar's visit will be more in the nature of 'talks about talks'. For two questions—the link between cross-border terrorism and the peace process as well as the role of Kashmir separatists—would need to be addressed to mutual satisfaction. In any event, the mere resumption of the dialogue is not going to lead to productive results.

The renewed political contact with Pakistan offers the foreign secretary the possibility of devising a new framework of engagement. Central to such a framework must be some shared political understanding among key stakeholders on both sides of the border. For no India-Pakistan dialogue is going to succeed without some clarity on the objectives and the will to negotiate compromises on stated positions. The significant change unfolding in the subcontinent—both within the region and in its international relations—demands that the two sides try and develop a fresh approach to the troubled relationship between India and Pakistan.

14 FEBRUARY 2015

Afghanistan: Avoiding Pak Rivalry

The logic of geography demands India recognise Pakistan's centrality in shaping the outcomes in Afghanistan.

With America ending the combat role of its armed forces in Afghanistan, Delhi's Kabul policy will be tested severely in 2015 and beyond. As Pakistan becomes, once again, the most important external actor in Afghanistan, Prime Minister Narendra Modi should resist the temptation to compete with Rawalpindi across the Durand Line. America's hopes that Afghanistan would be a more secure place than it was at the beginning of the Obama Administration in 2009, when Washington dramatically raised its military presence, have begun to fade. Amidst the resurgence of the Taliban, which has sanctuaries in Pakistan, Afghan forces have had one of the worst casualty and desertion rates this year. Kabul has barely managed to organise an orderly succession after the new republic's first president, Hamid Karzai, finished his second term. America's attempt to promote a political reconciliation between Kabul and the Taliban was a spectacular failure. The fanciful idea that putting all of Afghanistan's neighbours in one room might produce a regional peace framework never really had a chance. Matters will certainly come to a head when the Afghan forces face an all-out Taliban offensive to retake Kabul. Until then we should see an intense diplomatic play, with the Pakistan army at the centre stage.

Raheel Sharif, Pakistan's chief of army staff, says Rawalpindi wants to focus on the multiple internal challenges confronting Pakistan and needs stability on the western frontier. Sharif has also reached out to Kabul. The president of Afghanistan, Ashraf Ghani, is apparently ready to take Rawalpindi's words seriously, at least for the moment. After all there can be no peace in Afghanistan without some support from the Pakistan army. Many in India would scoff at General Sharif's sweet talk on Afghanistan and shake their head at American naiveté in falling for the same trick that every Pakistani general performs with such ease in Washington.

Realists in Delhi would say there is no reason to believe Rawalpindi will change its spots. Having invested so much blood and treasure over the decades to gain an enduring influence across the Durand Line, the Pakistan army is not about to turn a new leaf on Afghanistan. Delhi is probably right in believing that Rawalpindi is more likely to throw good money after bad in pursuit of 'strategic depth' in Afghanistan. But it should learn to hold its tongue. The doctrine of 'strategic depth' is not an invention of the Pakistan army but a legacy from the British Raj. When British India reached the Indus, the proponents of 'forward policy' suggested that Calcutta must look beyond the natural riverine border, seek influence in the tribal areas, and turn Afghanistan into a strategic buffer against European rivals. This turned out to be a costly policy for the Raj, but Pakistan's security establishment adopted it lock, stock and barrel after the Partition.

Like the Raj, Rawalpindi believes Pakistan's security needs a pliable regime in Kabul and a less-than-sovereign Afghanistan. There is a problem, though. Pakistan, as the successor state on the north-western frontier, inherited the geography of the Raj but not its vast resources. Partition, therefore, has given Pakistan much power to disrupt Afghanistan but not enough to construct a stable order. This tragic story of the Great Game is unlikely to change in 2015. If Pakistan is hobbled by the inheritance of the forward policy, the subcontinent's post-Partition geography compels Delhi to adopt a different approach, whose lineage too goes back to the Raj. It is the school of 'masterly inactivity' that challenged the tenets of forward policy.

Originally propounded by Lord John Lawrence, who rose from a provincial official in Delhi and Punjab to become the viceroy in the mid-19th century, 'masterly inactivity' called for restraint across the Indus. 'Masterly inactivity' was certainly not about inaction as its name suggested. It was about the virtues of 'strategic patience'. It demanded constant vigil, sustained intelligence-gathering, and an engagement with all relevant actors across the frontier. Above all it was about conserving one's scarce resources and deploying them at the most appropriate moment and location.

These must precisely be the attributes of Delhi's policy towards Afghanistan at the new juncture in the nation's evolution. Delhi must not forget the tyranny of geography limits India's role there. Delhi is in no position to compete with Rawalpindi in Afghanistan. Nor can it dream of replacing American military power across the Durand Line. On its part, Delhi must welcome any dialogue between Kabul and

Rawalpindi. It must encourage good neighbourly relations between Pakistan and a united and sovereign Afghanistan. At the same time, Delhi must prepare for a 'Plan B' when things begin to go wrong, again, in the north-western marches of the subcontinent.

12 DECEMBER 2014

After America: A Sino-Pak Alliance in Afghanistan?

Might China replace America in Afghanistan?

As the American occupation of Afghanistan comes to an end, China is getting ready to play a significant role in a country that has seen many great powers bite the dust. Chinese premier Li Keqiang has said Beijing is ready to play a 'constructive role' in promoting national reconciliation and economic development in Afghanistan. Although China's articulation of its Afghan policy is understated, India must come to terms with one important transformation unfolding in the north-western subcontinent. Afghanistan, which has long been a contested zone among Euro-Atlantic powers, may now see an Asian power take the lead role in the Great Game. Delhi must also recognise that there is widespread international and regional support for Beijing's strategic entry into Afghanistan. Kabul has been urging China to take greater interest in Afghanistan for many years now. Former president Hamid Karzai travelled frequently to Beijing to press the Chinese leadership to launch big development projects and persuade its close ally Pakistan to stop destabilising Kabul. His successor, Ashraf Ghani, who has chosen Beijing as his first foreign destination after he took charge of Afghanistan in September 2014, is betting on China to secure the nation's future.

Exhausted by its longest war ever, America has ended its combat role in Afghanistan in December 2014. Almost all of its remaining 10,000-odd troops in the country are likely to go home by the end of 2016. The US and its NATO allies are more than happy to see someone else pick up the pieces in Afghanistan. Russia, which is one of Beijing's major political partners, supports a stronger role for China in Afghanistan. China has good relations with most of Afghanistan's neighbours, including Iran and the three Central Asian Republics—Tajikistan, Uzbekistan and Turkmenistan. But it is Beijing's emerging partnership with the Pakistan army in Afghanistan that is the most interesting new element in the region.

Post-Partition geography has made Pakistan the most important regional actor in Afghanistan. Despite its best efforts, the Pakistan army could not gain a decisive say in Afghan affairs. Given its limited national resources, Rawalpindi's reach always exceeded its grasp in Afghanistan. But in alignment with a great power, Pakistan has had great impact there. After the Soviet occupation of Afghanistan at the end of 1979, the Pakistan army joined America in setting up the jihad against godless communists and ousting the Russian troops by the end of the 1980s. But Pakistan found it hard to control the developments in Afghanistan after the US turned its back on Afghanistan in the 1990s. America drafted Pakistan into the Great War on terror after the 9/11 attacks on Washington and New York in 2011. This time the US 'alliance' with Pakistan was a forced one. It was based on America's threat to bomb Pakistan to the Stone Age rather than a convergence of interests.

Pakistan waited patiently to undermine American strategy in Afghanistan. As it sees off the Americans, Pakistan is drawing China in to achieve its long-term strategic goal of establishing a friendly regime in Afghanistan and a special say in Kabul's internal affairs. On its part, Beijing hopes that collaboration with the Pakistan army in Afghanistan will help weaken the negative forces of violent extremism, religious fundamentalism and separatism that threaten China's internal security, especially in the restive Muslim majority province of Xinjiang. China values the geographic centrality of Afghanistan in promoting trans-border economic linkages between western China, Central Asia, the Persian Gulf and the subcontinent. A stable Af-Pak region, Beijing believes, can help consolidate China's 'Go-West' strategy and strengthen its influence in inner Asia.

As Americans began packing their bags in Afghanistan, China stepped up its regional diplomacy. While strengthening ties with Kabul, Beijing has established direct contacts with the Taliban with the help of the Pakistan army. Beijing is apparently ready to 'facilitate' a conversation among all the Afghan factions. Beijing has plans to extend its ambitious silk road initiative to cover Afghanistan and integrate it with the project to develop the China–Pakistan corridor. The biggest imponderable, however, remains the Taliban. It has set near impossible conditions for the peace process—the withdrawal of all foreigners from the country, ending Kabul's military partnerships with foreign powers and the imposition of Sharia. In the past, the development incentives offered by outsiders did not make a difference to Taliban's worldview. Many in Pakistan say the Taliban has changed and is ready for pragmatic engagement with the world. For China, though, the proof of the pudding will be in the eating. Rawalpindi's capacity to reorient the Taliban holds the key to a potentially successful Chinese role in Afghanistan.

17 DECEMBER 2014

Modi's engagement with Pakistan has revealed the familiar volatility in the bilateral relations. What began on a positive note when he sat down with Nawaz Sharif on his first day in office turned chilly and acrimonious within weeks. Six months after suspending talks with Pakistan, the Modi government began an effort to revive the dialogue in February 2015. But going by the pattern of past engagement, the last word has not been heard on how Modi's approach to Pakistan might evolve. He has signalled India's readiness to deepen economic ties but has insisted that talks can't go on if Pakistan supports terrorism. Modi's predecessors have said this before but returned sooner rather than later for talks despite the lack of satisfactory Pakistani action on terrorism. Modi has had to do the same.

If he is making a bold attempt changing the terms of engagement with Pakistan, Modi has to come to terms with the increasing constraints on India's role in Afghanistan. While Delhi has had a great run in Afghanistan since 2002, the withdrawal of US forces from Afghanistan and the prospects for renewed civil war in the nation make it difficult to sustain India's expansive economic engagement with Kabul. At the same time, Pakistan's growing weight in Afghan affairs and China's incipient role are also likely to limit Delhi's security cooperation with Kabul. The resurgence of the Taliban in Afghanistan and growing strength of the extremist forces in Pakistan would suggest the north-western marches of the subcontinent will remain India's greatest vulnerability through Modi's tenure as PM.

CHAPTER FIVE

Rethinking China

On China, Prime Minister Narendra Modi inherited a complex dynamic of stalled boundary negotiations, renewed tensions on the long and contested frontier, and an expanding trade deficit. Worse still, the gap between India and China—in the economic and defence domains—continued to widen. By the time Modi took charge, Beijing's GDP and annual defence spending were nearly four times those of Delhi. Modi was also faced with China's growing leverage in the subcontinent and the Indian Ocean that Delhi had long viewed as its sphere of influence. As the second largest economy and an aspiring superpower, China was also building new institutions and changing many existing ones.

Modi, who talked of China's 'expansionist mindset' during the election, was eager to engage China once he became the PM. So was Beijing eager to engage him, deeply impressed by his victory and hoping that Modi would extend his 'Gujarat model' to the rest of the nation and accelerate India's economic development. Modi did not allow the tensions on the border to overshadow President Xi Jinping's visit to India in September and initiated steps towards greater economic partnership with China. The columns in this chapter put into perspective the emergence of a new China policy in Delhi under Modi, who does not carry the defensive baggage from the past and has first-hand experience of doing business with Chinese companies in Gujarat.

The UPA Record

After multiple rounds, boundary talks with Beijing came back to square one under the UPA government.

The Manmohan Singh government sought to build on Atal Bihari Vajpayee's quest to find a political settlement to the boundary dispute with China through empowered 'Special Representatives'. The UPA government had early success in the form of an agreement in 2005 on the political parameters and guiding principles of a possible settlement. Since then, the boundary negotiations have made little progress on completing the second stage of the negotiations—finding a mutually acceptable territorial compromise on the long and contested border. The Special Representatives have had to shift their focus to the management of the recurring crises on the boundary. Their talks have helped devise a range of new mechanisms for promoting peace and tranquillity on the border. These include a working mechanism on border consultation and a border defence cooperation agreement. After a decade of boundary negotiations, then, India and China are back to managing the boundary dispute rather than resolving it. The mechanism of Special Representatives, created expressly for the purpose of boundary negotiations, has become a forum for general discussion of bilateral relations as well as the regional and international context.

When the next government reviews the UPA government's record of boundary negotiations with China, it will recognise two important factors that have made the resolution of the boundary dispute difficult. One is the changed military balance on the ground in Beijing's favour, thanks to the rapid modernisation of the Chinese military. Of particular significance has been China's large and consequential investment in transforming its logistical infrastructure on the Indo-Tibetan border. The UPA government has struggled to catch up with the upgradation of Indian infrastructure along and across a more difficult terrain. It is really up to the next government in Delhi to inject some speed and purpose into this important enterprise.

A second factor that has cast a shadow over India's negotiations with China has been the new dynamism in great power relations. In the middle of the last decade, China's relations with the US and Japan were in relative harmony and Delhi seemed entirely marginal to the Asian balance of power. That has begun to change amidst China's assertive regional posture, the US military rebalance to Asia and the mounting tensions between Beijing and Tokyo. India's warming relations with the US and Japan, however, have added to the complexity of Sino-Indian relations.

If there was an expectation that Beijing's difficult relations with Washington and Tokyo might lead to greater flexibility in China's negotiating position on the border dispute with India, it has not materialised. Relations between India and China have always been sensitive to the vagaries of their ties to third parties, including Pakistan, the Soviet Union and the US. Delhi will need considerable finesse in managing the impact of the great power dynamic and important third parties on its engagement with Beijing.

12 FEBRUARY 2014

China's Silk Routes

India must consider collaborating with China on large transborder projects.

As China reconfigures India's neighbourhood through its active promotion of new silk routes—over the Great Himalayas and across the Indian Ocean—New Delhi must make up its mind on how best to respond. Delhi is finding it hard to shed its defensiveness on the Chinese proposal for the so-called BCIM Corridor that will integrate eastern India, Bangladesh, Myanmar and south-western China. Delhi is even more suspicious of Beijing's invitation to join China in developing a 'maritime silk route' between the Pacific and Indian oceans. The reluctance in Delhi's foreign and security establishments against any overland connectivity projects with Beijing has been deep and is tied to the difficult political relationship and unresolved boundary dispute. Delhi has also been wary of China's growing maritime presence in the Indian Ocean, which it sees as India's backyard.

While Delhi fretted, China has expanded its connectivity over land and sea with India's neighbours in the subcontinent in the new century. In the north, China built the spectacular Tibet Railway to Lhasa and is planning to extend it to Nepal. To the east, Beijing plans to build road and rail connections to Bangladesh through Myanmar. China has built a twin pipeline system that will move oil and natural gas from Myanmar's Arakan coast to the Yunnan province. It also has plans to build a road and rail corridor parallel to the pipelines. In the west, China is modernising the trans-Karakoram highway, linking China's Xinjiang province and Pakistan's northern territories. It is now ready to invest billions of dollars to develop what is being called the 'Kashgar Corridor' that will connect Xinjiang province with the Arabian Sea. In the south, China has built new ports in Hambantota, Sri Lanka, and Gwadar, Pakistan. As its economic interests grow rapidly in the Indian Ocean, Beijing is also looking to develop maritime infrastructure all across the littoral as part of a new maritime silk route. Together, the Chinese projects compel us to rethink our long-held assumptions about India's physical space. The Great Himalayas are no longer a protective barrier for the subcontinent, as Chinese economic power now radiates out of inner Asia and connects markets and peoples that were once considered remote.

In the Indian Ocean, we have focused for centuries on Western primacy. As China becomes the world's foremost trading nation with an increasingly powerful navy, Beijing is all set to redefine India's maritime environment. President Xi Jinping has brought an extra edge to these gigantic connectivity projects that go under the name 'one belt, one road'. In its bold effort to re-engineer the subcontinent's physical environment, Beijing is behaving much like the British Raj, which sought to open new trade routes between India and inner Asia and develop connectivity with Xinjiang, Tibet and Yunnan. The difference, of course, is in the scale of the resources that China can mobilise today. If Beijing is reviving the Raj tradition, Delhi has largely forgotten it. If Partition physically shrunk India and separated it from many adjoining regions, an inward-looking economic policy devalued external transport corridors.

India has finally woken up in recent years to the implications of Chinese infrastructure projects in the subcontinent and beyond. Although Delhi now mutters the mantra of connectivity, its ability to turn words into deeds has been less than impressive. In responding to China's silk route development around the subcontinent and the Indian Ocean, Delhi must discard any residual notion that it can build a 'great wall' against Chinese economic influence in its neighbourhood. Nor should India believe economic cooperation with China will in itself help resolve Delhi's other political disputes with Beijing. Delhi needs to outline a bold vision for connectivity in India's frontier regions and across borders and identify a set of ambitious projects. If China can be useful in implementing some of them, Delhi must go ahead without any political hesitation. For India, China is not the only option. Japan has been eager to build corridors between India and South-East Asia. Multilateral institutions like the Asian Development Bank have long been eager to develop transborder projects between India and its neighbours. It is Delhi that has fallen short until now in the geo-economic reimagination of its region.

19 FEBRUARY 2014

A Modi Twist on China?

Can Modi mobilise the arts of Jujitsu to cope with China's challenge in the subcontinent?

Narendra Modi is in a position to give a new strategic twist to the Great Game tradition that has long animated India's foreign policy. Under the Raj, the Great Game was about ensuring the geopolitical unity of the subcontinent and preventing other powers from meddling in the region's internal affairs. The Partition, the Cold War and progressive economic isolation complicated Delhi's efforts to sustain the Great Game legacy in the decades after Independence. The steady expansion of the Indian economy and the slow accretion of military capabilities since the turn of the century have improved Delhi's ability to shape the subcontinent's strategic environment. But there are new challenges and none more important than the rise of China. The scale of this challenge on India's land frontiers to the north and the maritime frontier to the south is unlike anything modern India had to deal with in the past. During the 19th and early 20th centuries, threats from European powers like France, Russia and Germany dominated security planning under the Raj. After Independence, India bristled at Western involvement in India's neighbourhood, for example, the US's military cooperation with Pakistan.

Unlike Western powers, which are geographically distant and whose interest in the subcontinent is episodic, China is right next door and has long pushed for a greater role south of the Great Himalayas. It is also the world's second largest economy. As the West weakens and withdraws from India's neighbourhood and China becomes the most important external power in the subcontinent, there is no way Modi can play the Great Game by the old rules.

Instead, he must devise new ways of sustaining India's natural primacy in the subcontinent.

Central to Delhi's new strategic imagination must be the transformation of India's own relations with its neighbours. An India that can't stop quarrelling with its smaller neighbours only paves the way for an ever-larger Chinese role in the subcontinent. Equally important is India's need to come to terms with the reality of Chinese economic power. Whether it likes it or not, India can't really keep China out of the subcontinent. Instead of resisting China's growing economic weight, Delhi must turn it to India's advantage. One way of doing so is to discard the current inhibitions about China's investments and leverage Beijing's economic power to accelerate India's economic growth. For another, Delhi must stop whining about Beijing's mega projects in India's neighbourhood—from ports in Gwadar (Pakistan) and Hambantota (Sri Lanka) to oil and gas pipelines in Myanmar.

China's capacity to develop infrastructure projects is extraordinary and there is little point in fretting about it. Among the many significant Chinese projects in the region is the agreement to build the orange line of the Lahore metro and an offer to develop a deep sea port at the Sonadia Island in Bangladesh. The prime minister of Bangladesh, Sheikh Hasina, is sensitive to India's concerns about letting China build this port, but is eager to get on with the $10 billion project that will transform the upper Bay of Bengal. She has proposed the creation of a consortium of companies from Bangladesh, China and India to develop the Sonadia port. Beijing has signalled its readiness to work with India on this project. It is time India backed the consortium approach to regional infrastructure development and worked with all external powers, including China.

When Beijing sought support for developing the BCIM Corridor, the UPA government proposed an official study of the concept. But here is the big question: If China is ready to help India reintegrate the subcontinent, why is India resorting to delaying tactics? The answer is simple: because Delhi has been afraid of amending the rules of the Great Game.

7 JUNE 2014

Panchsheel Blues

China and India may have adhered to Panchsheel more in the breach rather than in observance.

As China and India mark the 60th anniversary of the Panchsheel—or the five principles of peaceful coexistence—unveiled by Prime Ministers Zhou Enlai and Jawaharlal Nehru in 1954, discerning observers ask one important question: why are all the celebrations taking place only in Beijing? Put simply, the truth is that India has long been ambivalent about Panchsheel. Many Indians view Panchsheel as a major 'discovery' of new principles of international relations—non-intervention in internal affairs of nations and peaceful coexistence. For some others, Panchsheel is the best example of Jawaharlal Nehru's idealist folly.

The five principles first made their appearance in Indian diplomacy as a preamble to an agreement that Delhi signed with Beijing in April 1954 on transborder trade and cultural engagement between India and the Tibet region of China. For its part, India had to come to terms with the changed political conditions in Tibet. In the decades before China gained control over Tibet, it was the British Raj that exercised primacy in the region. For centuries before the Raj, India and Tibet were bound by a shared culture and commerce.

The 1954 agreement came at the peak of the 'Hindi-Chini Bhai-Bhai' phase in bilateral relations. Five years later, Delhi and Beijing began to squabble over Tibet and fought a brief war in late 1962. Nehru was unwilling to renew the 1954 agreement, which lapsed after eight years in early 1962. Speaking a few years after Nehru's death, his close confidant and defence minister Krishna Menon criticised the deification of the five principles. He insisted that Panchsheel 'was not a revelation. It was not a creed or part of the formulation of our foreign policy'. If Panchsheel, in Menon's words, became 'a mantra, slogan and a prop' for India, it was very central to communist China's worldview. The essence of the five principles figured prominently in Mao Zedong's proclamation of the new republic on 1 October 1949. Mao was cautioning the West against intervention and reassuring it that the new China would not destabilise Asia.

When it came to India, the five principles had great salience, for Mao had no reason to accept Delhi's special relationship with Tibet and the multiple privileges that the government of India had inherited from the Raj. For Mao and his able premier, Zhou Enlai, the Panchsheel was about getting India to accept, unambiguously, Chinese sovereignty over Tibet. Ironically, China and India may have adhered to Panchsheel more in the breach rather than in observance. Beijing has often accused Delhi of meddling in Tibet, and Delhi has frequently fulminated at Beijing's support to secessionist movements in the North-East and beyond.

What keeps China and India away from excessive intervention in each other's internal affairs today is political prudence and not high principle. Delhi and Beijing know they can hurt each other by playing the secessionist card; therefore, both of them have the incentive to keep their involvement below the other's threshold of tolerance. While rhetoric is common in diplomacy, India and China might want to look beyond Panchsheel formalism and explore the prospects for expanding overland commerce and contact with China. After all, the 1954 agreement allowed customary transborder intercourse between India and Tibet. It permitted local traders and pilgrims to travel across the border without passports and visas. Those positive elements of the 1954 agreement have long been forgotten amidst the hype on Panchsheel. Instead of vacuous rhetoric on Panchsheel, Delhi must offer a vision of its own for a productive engagement with Beijing all across the Tibetan frontier. For one, Delhi and Beijing could agree to modernise the infrastructure at the Nathu La pass connecting Tibet and Sikkim and initiate full-fledged trade. They could also find ways to expand the current limited opportunities for Hindu and Buddhist pilgrims who want to visit places of worship on both sides of the border. The Narendra Modi government should be particularly interested in a significant expansion of Indian access to the holy sites of Kailash Manasarovar.

25 JUNE 2014

Asia for Asians: Xi Jinping's New Pitch

This kind of rhetoric has not been heard in Asia for decades.

As it rises to become a great power, China is determined to reconstitute Asian geopolitics, which had been dominated by the United States since the end of World War II. Central to Xi's argument is the proposition that the US security role in Asia is a manifestation of outmoded Cold War thinking. He is suggesting that American alliances must be replaced by a new regional security order. Xi has affirmed that 'in the final analysis, it is for the people of Asia to run the affairs of Asia, solve the problems of Asia and uphold the security of Asia. The people of Asia have the capability and wisdom to achieve peace and stability in the region through enhanced cooperation'. Heady stuff indeed. This kind of rhetoric has not been heard in Asia for decades.

The idea of 'Asia for Asians' is of old provenance and has a record of repeated failures. Way back in 1940, imperial Japan called for a 'bloc of Asian nations led by the Japanese and free of Western Powers'. If Tokyo's call found some political resonance among those Asians yoked to the European empires, Japan's own colonial ambitions exposed the limitations of the slogan 'Asia for Asians'. In fact, nationalist China, British India and the US pooled their resources to defeat Japanese imperialism. In the immediate post-war period, the idea of 'Asia for Asians' gathered much momentum after Nehru convened the Asian Relations Conference in early 1947. Yet the impact of the Cold War and new nationalisms in Asia undermined the hopes for Asian unity. As it normalised relations with the US in the 1970s, Beijing toned down its campaign against the American military presence in

Asia. It believed American alliances in Asia would counter 'Soviet hegemonism' and prevent the revival of 'Japanese militarism'.

China now appears confident that an America in decline has opened the door for the construction of a new security order in Asia. Xi's vigorous pursuit of 'Asia for Asians', however, has run into some political resistance. China's expanding military clout and its assertiveness in territorial disputes are driving some of its neighbours into a tighter embrace with the US. Although Xi has repeatedly sought to give the reassurance that China's rise is peaceful and Beijing will never exercise hegemony, few Asians are willing to take it at face value. Quite the contrary. In Tokyo, Prime Minister Shinzo Abe has decided to re-interpret Japan's peace constitution. After being a passive partner in the military alliance with the US all these decades, Tokyo is seeking a more active military role in shaping its security environment. Communist Vietnam, which fought a bitter war against the US in the 1960s and 1970s, has rapidly expanded its security cooperation with Washington. The Philippines, which threw American military forces out of the country in the early 1990s, is restoring the American presence and deepening defence ties with Japan.

If Beijing is trying to undermine American alliances in Asia, its neighbours are trying to strengthen them. How does India respond to this unfolding contestation in Asia? On the face of it, a non-aligned India should oppose all alliances and support collective security proposals seemingly in tune with Delhi's 'idealist' tradition. Yet, India's foreign policy record speaks otherwise. After its conflict with China in 1962, India turned first to the US and then the Soviet Union to balance Beijing. Despite its embrace of Moscow, Delhi rejected the proposals for collective security that emanated from Russia's Leonid Brezhnev (1969) and Mikhail Gorbachev (1986). Put simply, non-aligned India was not averse to playing balance of power politics when compelled by external circumstances.

As an increasingly powerful China seeks to reorder Asia, Delhi must firmly locate China's Panchsheel campaign in a clinical assessment of Asia's rapidly evolving geopolitics and its consequences for Indian security. China is doing what rising powers, including the US, have done before—frame one's national interests in universal terms, push other major powers out of one's immediate vicinity and replace the old regional order with a new one. Beijing is undoubtedly following a well-trodden path in international politics. But Delhi appears a long way from developing an appropriate strategy to cope with Asia's new power play.

4 JULY 2014

Sabarmati Summit

Modi's focus on attracting Chinese investments could help Delhi get out of the current deadlock with Beijing.

In receiving Chinese president Xi Jinping in Ahmedabad in September and hosting a private dinner for him on the banks of the Sabarmati river, Narendra Modi has begun to break the mould of Indian diplomacy towards China. For too long, India's summit-level engagement with China has been too formal, with little space for relaxed conversation. With Modi at the helm in New Delhi for five years and Xi slated to rule China for nine, it made sense to add a touch of political informality and personal intimacy to the interaction between the two leaderships. China's political investment in Modi when he was chief minister of Gujarat, at a time when America and Europe were unwilling to touch him with a bargepole, has generated rare personal goodwill for Beijing with an Indian leader. The ease of doing business in Gujarat during Modi's tenure saw many Chinese companies set up shop in the state. Since his election as prime minister, the Chinese media has written glowingly about the 'Gujarat model' of economic development and the likelihood of its extension to the rest of the country.

China is also conscious of the fact that Modi is the first Indian leader since Rajiv Gandhi to have a majority in the Lok Sabha and the popularity at home to address difficult issues in bilateral relations and seize the possibilities for changing the nature of the ties. Beijing recognises that Delhi's political will has been burnished under Modi and is willing to overlook, at least for the moment, the PM's statements on 'Chinese expansionism' and his outreach to Japan and the United States. In agreeing to spend time with Modi on his birthday in Gujarat, Xi is signalling that he is ready to build a long-term personal relationship with the Indian PM.

Hard-nosed realists around the world are impressed with Modi's diplomatic flair seen during his visits to Nepal and Japan. But they ask if Modi can go beyond the atmospherics and bring about a substantial change in the relationship with China. In his address to Japanese businessmen in Tokyo in September 2014, Modi declared that he is a Gujarati and commerce runs in his blood. This emphasis on commercial pragmatism and deal-making may help Modi get India out of its current deadlock with China.

Consider, for example, the contradictions that Modi has inherited on China: India has traditionally employed grandiose political rhetoric that talked of heralding the Asian century and transforming the world order in collaboration with China. This soaring rhetoric on abstract goals was accompanied by a reluctance to openly acknowledge and discuss differences with China on a range of bilateral and regional issues. Delhi also finds it hard to do such simple things as liberalising the visa regime for Chinese businessmen, journalists and scholars. Delhi does not let Beijing set up more cultural centres in India. And when it came to Chinese investments in India, Delhi found multiple ways of saying 'no'. Delhi has also been reluctant to open up overland trade corridors across the Great Himalayas in the north or the east.

It is not that there are no problems associated with all these issues, but they all could be resolved with political will. Modi's self-assurance, it is possible to imagine, will help Delhi craft a new approach to Beijing that will let India stand firm on core national security concerns and yet be practical in widening the areas of economic cooperation. In inviting massive Chinese investments across a wide range of sectors, Modi might be opening the door for a new policy towards China. While Modi might be tempted to use the rhetoric of his predecessors, he should recognise that building a new world order with China could wait for the moment. For now, the priority must be to leverage the Chinese economic strength to accelerate India's own growth.

In seeking greater Chinese participation in the Indian economy, Modi would only emulate China's pragmatism. Despite the Japanese occupation of China in the 1930s and 1940s, Beijing eagerly sought Japanese investments to build modern China after initiating reforms in 1978. Just two decades after fighting the costly Korean War (1950–53) with the US, China warmed up politically to Washington in the 1970s and has benefited immensely from economic cooperation with America since the late 1970s.

Deepening commercial engagement with China may not necessarily lead to either the resolution of the boundary dispute that continues to hobble the bilateral relationship or end Delhi's growing competition with Beijing for strategic influence in the Indo-Pacific. Modi could walk and chew gum at the same time; he could grow business ties with China while addressing simultaneously the multiple political contentions with Beijing.

17 SEPTEMBER 2014

China Rising in South Asia

Modi confronts a new reality in the subcontinent: China is now the most important external economic power in South Asia.

India's challenge of coping with China's growing economic weight in the subcontinent is far more demanding than dealing with its military power. The problem of closing the military gap with China is not a hard one to think through. It involves accelerating India's own military modernisation, developing a strategy to deter Beijing's potential aggression on the long-disputed border and increasing security partnerships with other great powers. But Delhi is acutely conscious that it is Beijing's rising economic profile in the subcontinent that will have major long-term consequences for the regional balance of power between India and China. Yet there is no way Delhi can exclude Beijing, the world's second largest economic power, from its own calculus for accelerating India's economic development. If the Manmohan Singh government sent out ambiguous signals on economic cooperation with China, Modi appears determined to advance the bilateral economic cooperation with Beijing. Modi is eager to mobilise Chinese technology, capital and organisational skills to promote his agenda of infrastructure development and manufacturing at home.

Long used to a black-and-white approach to international affairs, Delhi is struggling to find a dual track policy towards Beijing—competing with it for strategic influence and at the same time strengthening economic cooperation with China. This problem gets magnified at the regional level. India has long objected to military cooperation between China and South Asian nations. However, Delhi is in no credible position to oppose commercial cooperation between Beijing and its subcontinental neighbours, because it sees China as a major economic partner at the bilateral and global level. To make matters more complicated, Beijing is not seeking exclusive bilateral economic engagement with India's neighbours but wants Delhi to be an active regional partner through trilateral, quadrilateral and multilateral mechanisms. Beijing does not present itself as a rival to Delhi in South Asia but as a great power that is willing to deal with everyone in the region, including Delhi, with a positive approach ready to patiently work through the regional contradictions.

If China is smothering the region with its version of the power of positive thinking, India appears paralysed by the fear of transborder economic collaboration with Beijing. Delhi's security establishment, which continues to think of the subcontinent as India's exclusive sphere of influence, has a hard time imagining its neighbours as commercial bridges to China. Delhi's economic decision makers with their inward orientation appear to have no capacity to think of a strategy of regional integration in partnership with China, or any other great power. The Foreign Office's conservatism on China means its current focus is on fobbing off Chinese proposals through public silence and private rejection. India is quite unready to adjust its mental maps to the structural shift in its regional environment. The longer India takes to adapt, the greater will be the negative consequences for India's regional standing. It is really up to Modi to press the system to come up with a comprehensive strategy to deal with the opportunities and challenges presented by the rise of Chinese economic power on India's frontiers. In the interim, Modi must agree to take up one or two joint commercial projects with China in Nepal and Bangladesh to test out the prospects for a regional partnership with Beijing.

3 JANUARY 2015

Between the US and China

Modi signals the confidence to engage both Washington and Beijing.

Modi's decision to expand the engagement with the United States on regional security in the Asia Pacific and the Indian Ocean during President Obama's visit to India has set off much hand wringing in Delhi's foreign community about the potential Chinese reaction. These fears are not new and are rooted in Delhi's lack of strategic self-assurance. Any careful assessment of China's foreign policy record or its current geopolitical calculus would suggest these fears are misplaced. Consider, for example, the fact that China had been closer over extended periods of time to Washington than India has ever been to America in the last seven decades. Even today, China's economic and commercial relationship is much thicker than Delhi's ties with either Washington or Beijing. If India's trade with the US and China stands at around $100 billion and $70 billion respectively, China–US trade now stands at $560 billion. Even America's Asian allies, including Japan, South Korea and Australia, have dense relations with China.

Instead of viewing its relations with Washington and Beijing in binary terms, Delhi must recognise that its relations with both America and China are way below potential and need to be developed with greater purpose. China, of course, does not limit its partnership with America by citing concerns of its large neighbours like Russia, Japan and India. Beijing, in fact, is urging the United States to agree to a 'new type of great power relations' with China that could generate a shared leadership between the two giants. Beijing uses its relationship with America to secure its own national interests, shape the global balance of power and reshape its regional environment. India must try and do the same.

The idea that Beijing will react violently to India's engagement with America is also not borne out by the history of Sino-Pak relations. After all, Pakistan has been a strong military partner for both America and China. Pakistan joined the US military alliance system in the 1950s, including the Central Treaty Organisation and the South East Asia Treaty Organisation, at a time when America was determined to combat communism in Asia and did not recognise the People's Republic of China. The military alliance with America did not prevent Pakistan from warming up to China in the 1950s. Unlike India, where the hot air about non-alignment began to introduce ideological rigidity and strategic incoherence into India's foreign policy, Pakistan thought more creatively about the possibilities with

America and China. Navigating the complex dynamic between Washington and Beijing in the 1950s and 1960s, Pakistan became a valuable bridge between America and China when the two sides wanted to normalise relations at the turn of the 1970s. China did not object to intense military partnership between America and Pakistan in the 1980s or when Washington declared that Rawalpindi is a 'major non-NATO ally' in the 2000s.

Whatever concerns that the Chinese leaders might have on the future of India's relations with America, their focus for now is on downplaying contradictions with India and finding common ground between Beijing and Delhi. For China has enough problems in Asia, especially in its East Asian front yard. Nor have China's differences with America become irreconcilable. Not yet. The Chinese foreign minister, Wang Yi, was quite calm in responding to questions from reporters about Obama's visit to India. 'India has its relationship with the US; we have our own,' Wang said. 'As a good friend of India,' Wang added, 'we want India to make friends everywhere.'

Wang underlined Beijing's strong commitment to expand the cooperative engagement with the Modi government. Much in the manner that Washington values a purposeful regime in Delhi that is capable of doing deals, Beijing too is eager to advance on a wide range of issues with the Modi government. With neither America nor China asking India to choose between them, the Modi government is in a good position to strengthen its cooperation with both and boost India's comprehensive national power. It is India's strategic community that must learn to discard the traditional binaries in its foreign policy discourse—either America or China, and alignment versus non-alignment.

There is no reason too for India to maintain equal distance between the world's two greatest powers. There will be some issues on which

India will be closer to America—for example, on how to reduce tensions in the South China Sea. On others, like non-intervention in the internal affairs of third countries, Delhi would like to sit in Beijing's corner. India's expanding engagement with China and the United States does not mean they will evolve either symmetrically or at the same pace. For example, on the economic front, China could be the preferred partner in some sectors like physical infrastructure development. The US partnership is critical for the development of India's knowledge-based industries. On security issues, America is a distant power with which India has no direct disputes. China, on the other hand, is a large neighbour whose power is growing rapidly. India has big problems with China, including a long and contested boundary. India's security partnership with America flows naturally from the logic of geopolitics. But how far Delhi might go with Washington would depend upon its assessment of the security threats from Beijing.

30 JANUARY 2015

Modi's first year in office has brought into view a new five-fold policy—a pragmatic version of the Panchsheel, as it were—in dealing with China. One, Delhi is not going to sweep under the carpet the problem of mounting tensions on the contested boundary and is ready to take on a more assertive posture in patrolling the disputed frontiers with China. At the same time, Modi is suggesting India is ready to explore 'out-of-the-box' solutions to the boundary dispute. Two, to improve India's deterrent capabilities, the Modi government is accelerating India's defence modernisation and upgrading the infrastructure on the border. Three, the Modi government is discarding some of Delhi's long-standing inhibitions about economic engagement with China and is making India more open to Chinese investments. Four, Modi is conscious of the challenge that China poses to India's primacy in the subcontinent. Delhi is also aware that it can't stop its neighbours from expanding engagement with the world's second largest economy. The focus is on accelerating its own economic and political cooperation with the neighbours by leveraging India's natural advantages in the region. Finally, Modi has been less hesitant than his predecessors in drawing close to America and its Asian allies to strengthen India's comprehensive national power and redress the growing gap between the strategic capabilities of Delhi and Beijing. Together these five principles provide the foundation for a very different approach to China than the one we have seen since the middle of the 20th century.

CHAPTER SIX

Embracing America

One of Modi's biggest surprises since he took charge as prime minister was his unhesitant embrace of the United States. For a leader who was denied entry to the US for nearly a decade by Washington, which cited his alleged role in the Gujarat riots of 2002, Modi was quite clear that his personal grievance and the pursuit of national interest must be kept separate. He was quick to respond to President Barack Obama's invitation to visit the US in September.

Modi's engagement with Obama was focused on ending the drift in India–US relations during the second term of the UPA government and injecting some fresh momentum into the bilateral relations. Modi's warm outreach to the US was also a break from the opportunistic opposition of the BJP leadership during the UPA rule to the historic civil nuclear initiative with the United States. Modi in contrast was clear in recognising the centrality of the US in promoting India's internal economic transformation and improving its international standing. The columns in this section assess the unexpected shifts in

India's thinking about the US and the potential for a genuine transformation under Modi.

Washington Is Ready for Modi

Is the US gearing up to discard its hostility towards Modi?

As the last round of polling closed in the Indian general elections during the middle of May 2014, the Obama Administration became the first foreign government to express its eagerness to work with Narendra Modi, widely expected to win the elections. In statements issued by the White House and the State Department, Washington offered fulsome praise for India's general elections, underlined the shared democratic values between the two nations, and affirmed Washington's political commitment to work with the new Prime Minister of India. Although the statements did not name Modi, their political intent was quite clear. Washington wants to put behind the controversy over the US denial of a visa for Modi since 2005. In the summer of 2014, Washington scrambled to make up in quick time. When the US kept its distance from Modi, Asian powers like China and Japan aggressively courted the Gujarat chief minister over the last decade. The British and West European governments, which had joined the US in criticising Modi in 2002, smartly got off the high horse when they sensed that the political prospects of the Gujarat chief minister at the national level could not be ignored.

It was only after Modi was declared the prime ministerial candidate of the BJP in early 2014 that the US asked its envoy in Delhi, Nancy

Powell, to call on the Gujarat CM. On his part, Modi has repeatedly stated during the election campaign that he is not going to allow any personal bitterness to come in the way of strengthening India's relations with the United States. Modi also chose to recall the proposition that India and the US are 'natural allies' that was first articulated by Prime Minister Atal Bihari Vajpayee in 1998 and became the basis for the transformation of Indo-US relations thereafter. Although Modi has said all the right things in the election campaign, Washington was acutely aware of the accumulated political damage done and the need for some visible warmth towards the new PM.

13 MAY 2014

The Washington Test

Seen from the perspective of Modi's campaign for prime ministership, the US is the Uttar Pradesh of India's international politics.

Prime Minister Narendra Modi's planned visit to Washington at the end of September 2014 is not just about restoring the lost dynamism in the engagement between Delhi and Washington under UPA 2. The outcomes from Modi's Washington sojourn are likely to shape the contours of India's global role at a time when renewed great power tensions are undermining international peace and breaking down the old order in Europe and Asia. Modi appears to have understood that the relationship with the US is too important to be left to the mercies of the conservative Foreign Office or his party cadre, which views diplomacy as another form of emotion. No wonder the PM rejected the calls to shun Washington until there was a formal apology from the US on the visa denial to Modi since 2005. Modi has made it clear that he has no personal grouse against Washington and that he will deal with the US on the basis of national interest. Seen from the perspective of Modi's campaign for prime ministership, the US is the Uttar Pradesh of international politics. If you get the world's biggest power right, your pursuit of larger political goals becomes that much easier. Modi has understood that the expansion of India's engagement with the US will significantly improve its room for manoeuvre with Pakistan, China, Europe, Japan and Russia.

Modi is not proclaiming some new principle but merely emulating Atal Bihari Vajpayee, who successfully cut through India's international isolation after the 1998 nuclear tests by pushing for a strategic partnership with the US. The UPA government forgot this principle and started deliberately distancing itself from Washington in the name of non-alignment. Modi need not align his government with the US against other powers. But, like Vajpayee, he must engage all the major powers, each on its own merit, and make cooperation with them an integral part of India's national development strategy.

30 JULY 2014

Modi's American Business

If UPA's economic drift undermined Delhi's foreign policy, Modi is determined to revive the story on India as an economic opportunity for American business.

Prime Minister Narendra Modi has wisely chosen to spend some quality time, both individually and collectively, with the leaders of American business in New York and Washington. If the perception of India as a major business opportunity since the reforms began a quarter of a century ago provided the basis for raising Delhi's diplomatic profile on the global stage, the economic drift in the second term of the UPA rule inevitably constrained India's room for foreign policy manoeuvre. Convincing American companies that India is back in business has been one of Modi's most important political objectives in the US.

As the most business-friendly prime minister India has ever had, Modi might be well placed to successfully pursue this task. Thanks to India's first prime minister, Jawaharlal Nehru, a thinly veiled contempt for capital is very much part of Delhi's political culture. Nehru, who kept India's businessmen at arm's length at home, made no secret of his distaste at having to deal with what he saw as excessive American materialism and a crass commercial culture during his first visit to the US in 1949. Modi is probably as 'non-Nehruvian' as you could get in India, at least on the relationship between private business and national strategy. Modi's finance minister, Arun Jaitley, in turn, has often said that there is no contradiction in being 'pro-poor' and 'pro-business' at the same time.

Delhi's current pro-business orientation marks a new stage in India's appreciation of the role of international capital in the conduct of the nation's foreign policy. For Nehru and Indira Gandhi, focused as they were on economic self-reliance, there was hardly any room for mixing international business and diplomacy. Rajiv Gandhi was the first prime minister who began to see the intrinsic connection between the two. But it was not easy changing the political culture of the Indian Foreign Service, which privileged political activity over the commercial. After all, the Indian diplomatic corps emerged out of the Indian Political Service of the pre-Independence period. Under the Raj, these officers proudly called themselves the 'politicals' as they engaged in high politics with the princely states in the subcontinent and the principalities on the periphery.

At the dawn of the reform era, P.V. Narasimha Rao began to take business delegations along with him to foreign capitals. He made a special effort to reach out to the business communities, especially in the US. In the early 1990s, for example, the Indian embassy in Washington encouraged the setting up of an 'India Interest Group' with leading companies like GE. This group helped Delhi block the anti-Indian resolutions on Kashmir and Punjab that were routinely passed in the US Congress, thanks to the uncontested lobbying by groups backed by Pakistan. India's political outreach in Washington was also reinforced by business associations like the CII (Confederation of Indian Industry) and the Federation of Indian Chambers of Commerce and Industry (FICCI).

In the Manmohan Singh years, bilateral CEO forums became an important tool in India's economic diplomacy. Soon, like everything else, its business diplomacy became an ineffective ritual. The slowdown in the country's economic growth and Delhi's policy paralysis over the last few years saw India lose credibility with the business leaders around the world. As part of his effort to accelerate India's economic growth, Modi has taken personal charge of

PTI

Prime Minister Narendra Modi has largely followed the foreign policy direction set by his predecessor, Manmohan Singh, but with greater vigour and purpose. Modi has also complemented that continuity with fresh initiatives and new priorities of his own.

As a relatively young and energetic mass leader, after many ageing prime ministers in Delhi since the 1990s, Modi has connected easily with people beyond India's borders, especially in the subcontinent. He is seen here wading into a crowd in Kathmandu during his visit to Nepal in August 2014.

PTI

AP

'With Pakistan if possible; without it if necessary.' Proclaiming the objective of shared prosperity, Modi pushed for a faster pace of regional economic integration in the subcontinent at the South Asian summit in Kathmandu in November 2014. He is seen here alongside Pakistan's prime minister, Nawaz Sharif.

PTI

Security cooperation with the island states is at the heart of Modi's Indian Ocean policy. He is seen here unveiling a coastal surveillance radar in the Seychelles during his Sagar Yatra in March 2015.

PTI

Modi is unabashed about displaying his personal religiosity in public during his diplomatic travels. As the first Indian prime minister in nearly 30 years to travel to Sri Lanka on a bilateral visit, he offered prayers at the Naguleswaram Temple near the northern town of Jaffna.

PTI

(above) Despite the opposition in his own party to the Land Boundary Agreement with Bangladesh, Modi has publicly committed to its ratification by Parliament as part of a strategic decision to transform relations with Dhaka. He is seen here with Prime Minister Sheikh Hasina.

PTI

(left) Modi never missed an opportunity during his international engagements to celebrate India's democratic values. He met Aung San Suu Kyi, leader of the opposition in Myanmar, on the margins of the East Asia Summit in Nay Pyi Taw in November 2014.

Reuters

PTI

(above) Modi has matched his determination to improve ties with America with an equally important attempt to cultivate non-Western allies. He is seen here with the leaders of Russia, Brazil, China and South Africa at the summit of the BRICS forum in Fortaleza, Brazil, in July 2014.

Modi's special effort to deepen the strategic partnership with Japan has been facilitated by his personal rapport built over the years with the Japanese prime minister, Shinzo Abe.

Reuters

Outreach to the diaspora has been one of the central themes of Modi's foreign policy. During his visit to the United States in September 2014, he got a rock star's reception at the spectacular gathering of the Indian-American community in New York's Madison Square Garden.

Reuters

In two quick summits between September 2014 and January 2015, Modi and US president Barack Obama ended the drift in bilateral relations, removed some of the obstacles to civil nuclear energy cooperation and unveiled an ambitious framework for strategic cooperation in the Indo-Pacific region. Modi is seen here welcoming Obama with a big hug when he broke protocol to personally receive him at the Delhi airport in January 2015.

PTI

In tune with the BJP's well-known warmth towards Israel, Modi has unveiled an enthusiastic engagement with Israel and lifted the veil of secrecy over a partnership that has steadily expanded since the early 1990s. He is seen here with the prime minister of Israel, Benjamin Netanyahu, at the United Nations General Assembly in September 2014.

Renuka Puri, *The Indian Express*

Despite the growing tensions between Russia and the West over Ukraine and his eagerness to elevate ties with the US, Modi has sustained Delhi's time-tested special relationship with Moscow. He is seen here with Russian president Vladimir Putin.

PTI

Improving relations with China has become a central plank of Modi's foreign policy. Lending a personal touch to the interaction with the Chinese leadership, he hosted President Xi Jinping in Ahmedabad in September 2014.

PTI

If India had problems with Australia and Canada during the Cold War, Modi has deepened ties with the two Commonwealth nations that welcome Indian migration, offer their rich natural resources and can help reinforce India's global political reach. He is seen here addressing the Indian diaspora in Sydney in November 2014.

India's engagement with international business. In recognising the importance of US business in the shaping of Washington's external policies, Modi is emulating China's strategy in America over the last three decades. Strong ties with American big business helped Beijing fend off bursts of political hostility in Washington. The rapid expansion of American commercial interests in China and the growing economic interdependence between the two countries today acts as the biggest countervailing force to the unfolding geopolitical tensions between the world's foremost powers.

On a smaller scale, India's own recent experience underlines the importance of engaging American business in pursuing the country's larger political goals in Washington. When President George W. Bush and Prime Minister Manmohan Singh unveiled the historic civil nuclear initiative, it was well understood that getting the approval of the US Congress would be an uphill task. It needed the full mobilisation of American businesses with an interest in India to persuade Congress to support exempting Delhi from the long-standing domestic laws and international rules on nuclear non-proliferation. The US companies saw the civil nuclear initiative as the key to unlock a stronger strategic and economic partnership with India, from which they would benefit significantly.

Close to a decade later, at the end of 2014, the nuclear deal remained in limbo. Although American arms sales to India have grown, it has not been easy for US companies to deal with the complex rules and procedures of the ministry of defence in Delhi. Worse still, American business has turned from ally to adversary, asking Congress and the Obama Administration to impose punitive measures on India by citing a range of Delhi policies, including those on IPR, trade, investment and taxation. On his part, Modi seems determined to reverse this negative turn in relations with American business, which has an important role to play in accelerating India's economic growth and revitalising Delhi's strategic partnership with Washington. Whether he can overcome the widespread American scepticism about investing in India and suggest pragmatic pathways to address the many economic disputes with the US are indeed the most interesting questions about Modi's journey to America.

25 SEPTEMBER 2014

Defensive No More

Modi is on a roll in New York.

Arriving in New York at the end of September 2014, Prime Minister Narendra Modi was on a political roll. The PM chatted with UN Secretary General Ban Ki-moon and addressed the UN General Assembly for the first time. A spectacular reception was planned for him by the Indian-American community at Madison Square Garden. He underlined India's shared interests with the US on combating violent extremism by visiting the memorial for the victims of 9/11, connected with leaders from India's neighbouring countries and met American mayors and governors. Modi is widely seen in America as India's most credible international interlocutor since Rajiv Gandhi, with the political will to turn India's long talked about economic and strategic potential into reality. But the visit to the US has also touched on Modi's Achilles heel: his controversial past in Gujarat. The outpouring of enthusiasm for him within the Indian-American community has overshadowed the smaller protest demonstrations against the PM but Modi's critics in America are not going away. Some of them have persuaded local courts to issue summons to him, citing his role during the 2002 Gujarat riots. As India's internal divisions manifest themselves in America, Washington has made it clear that Modi enjoys absolute immunity during his visit to the US. If America's political leadership is ready to embrace Modi, its business elite is eager to be persuaded that India is back in business; neither is interested in digging up his past.

At the UN General Assembly in New York, Modi refused to be drawn into a verbal brawl with Pakistan's Nawaz Sharif, who referred to the mid-20th century UN call for a plebiscite in Jammu and Kashmir a day before. Modi, instead, reaffirmed his desire for a dialogue with Pakistan and reminded Islamabad of its responsibility to create the right atmosphere. More importantly, he chose to focus on his larger foreign policy vision. Modi's UN speech has set the stage for a more productive engagement with the world by discarding India's recent defensiveness on multilateral issues—from terrorism to trade, and climate change to global commons. On all these, Modi has hinted at more innovative approaches on Delhi's part if the US is ready to address India's genuine concerns.

29 SEPTEMBER 2014

The Second Chance

Modi is shedding India's traditional diffidence towards America.

During his energetic tour of America, Modi has turned the gathering pessimism about India's relations with the US into an optimistic storyline. After Obama's visit to India in 2010, bilateral ties hit a plateau and headed soon enough to the south. In its first term, the UPA surprised the world with its openness to transforming the relationship with the US. In its second, it returned India to its bad old ways. Delhi signalled it was not open for political or economic business with America. It preferred to posture rather than engage on differences and was hesitant about building on the many possibilities for partnering with America that emerged. Above all, the UPA government was paralysed by an ideological ambivalence towards America.

Modi ran an impressive campaign of public diplomacy to mobilise the Indian-American community and the political classes in Washington in favour of rejuvenating the bilateral partnership. None of this was foreseen either in Delhi or in Washington. Coming from where he did, Modi, it was widely assumed, had little incentive to warm up to the US. His party, the BJP, had turned negative on America when it sat on the opposition benches during the decade-long rule of the UPA. It abandoned the legacy of Atal Bihari Vajpayee, who had declared that India and the US were natural allies, and joined hands with the CPM in opposing the civil nuclear initiative. On top of that, America made Modi a political untouchable by withdrawing his visa for ten long years. Indeed, many in Delhi argued that Modi should not travel to the US unless there was an apology from Washington.

In overruling these sentiments and taking the first opportunity to visit Washington, Modi recognised that expanding cooperation with the US is critical to effectively pursuing India's domestic development agenda as well as to raising its relative position in the world. The joint statement issued after his talks with Obama stated Modi's appreciation of the US unambiguously: 'Prime Minister Modi emphasised the priority India accords to its partnership with the US, a principal partner in the realisation of India's rise as a responsible, influential world power.' This thesis is certainly not new. The idea was first articulated by the Bush Administration in 2005, when it stated that it was in America's interest to assist India's rise to great power status. If there was much scoffing at this in the foreign policy establishment, the Congress virtually panicked at the thought of drawing close to the US. Even as he underlined the importance of American partnership in facilitating India's rise, celebrated shared democratic values and highlighted the common interests in the region and beyond, Modi set his own terms for an equitable and mutually beneficial relationship.

On the question of economic reform, Modi made it clear that he was going to do it his own way and was not going to simply tick off the American checklist. The PM promised to make it easy for Americans to invest and do business in India, and invited them to take commercial decisions on the basis of practical evaluation of the new possibilities in the country rather than an abstract discussion on reforms. Modi also brought a new pragmatism to resolving the multiple differences with the US. In the past, standing up to America had become a domestic political end in itself, whether it was trade, climate change or civil nuclear liability. India's past grandstanding was rooted in a lack of national self-confidence and the inability to assess its long-term interests at home and abroad. In contrast, Modi is saying a self-assured India is now ready to address difficult issues in a practical manner and on the basis of mutual give and take.

On geopolitics, too, Modi is shedding the traditional diffidence that marked India's engagement with the US. In South Asia, India has long been wary of American partnership with Pakistan and, more recently, of US dependence on Rawalpindi to secure its interests in Afghanistan. As the north-western marches of the subcontinent enter a more turbulent phase, Modi is eager to explore new opportunities for cooperation with the US in stabilising Afghanistan and in countering the sources of international terrorism in Pakistan. In Washington, Modi has been more vigorous than his predecessors in highlighting India's converging interests with America in East Asia. He is also a lot less hesitant about engaging the US in the Middle East, a region of vital economic interest and great political sensitivity for India.

Rekindling a romance is never easy. In 2005, when America unveiled a bold new approach towards India, Washington was at the apogee of the unipolar moment and Delhi was politically unprepared. A decade later, the US has greater stakes in India's success and Modi has brought much needed clarity to Delhi's strategic calculus on America. If the expansive agenda unveiled by Modi and Obama is matched by bureaucratic purposefulness in Delhi and Washington, India and America have a second chance at building a strategic partnership of considerable consequence.

2 OCTOBER 2014

Modi's R-Day Invite to Obama

Modi makes bold to invite Obama to be the chief guest at India's Republic Day celebrations in January 2015.

The presence of US president Barack Obama at India's Republic Day celebrations in January 2015 represents the long-awaited moment of transformation in India's relations with America and an extraordinary shift in Delhi's worldview. Prime Minister Modi's decision to invite Obama and the American president's acceptance reveal the scale and scope of the mutual understanding that appears to have emerged out of the meeting between the two leaders in September 2014. Modi and Obama appear poised to clinch a broad set of ambitious agreements—ranging from civil nuclear cooperation and defence at one end to economic agreements at the other—that will lay the foundation for a genuine strategic partnership between India and America.

That this is the first time Delhi has invited an American president to join the Republic Day celebrations highlights enduring Indian ambivalence towards the United States in the past. The reluctance of the world's largest democracy to share the most important day in its national life with the world's most powerful democracy underlined how estranged the two republics had become over the decades. It was indeed commonplace to suggest that anti-Americanism was deeply embedded within the DNA of the Indian political and bureaucratic classes. This jinx has now been broken by Modi.

That the news of the invitation to Obama came first from Modi's personal Twitter handle and not from either the Prime Minister's Office or the Ministry of External Affairs reveals the extraordinary personal attention that the PM has devoted to the relationship with America. The latest development takes us back to 2005–06, when

Bush offered a rare opportunity to Prime Minister Manmohan Singh to transform the partnership between the two countries. But self-doubt in the Congress leadership and opportunistic opposition from the BJP saw India squander that rare moment. With stronger authority over his own party and government and a clear vision of India's international goals, Modi is all set to pick up the ball that was dropped by the UPA government a decade ago. Although many in Delhi say Obama is a lame-duck president, Modi knows that the American president has considerable freedom to conduct foreign policy until the very last day in office and has immense executive power to effect change in the relations with India. Strong Republican support for India in the US Congress, the new tensions in America's ties with China and Russia, and the unfolding geopolitical flux in the Middle East and Asia make it possible for Modi and Obama to boldly re-imagine the bilateral partnership.

22 NOVEMBER 2014

Modi Rewrites the Script with Obama

Modi and Obama resolve outstanding differences and set new strategic goals.

Barack Obama's second visit to India as the American president began with a surprise when Modi chose to break protocol and personally receive the president at the airport about 24 hours before the 2015 Republic Day celebrations began. The PM's moves during the course of the day included a decisive resolution of some of the outstanding issues with America. Modi also set new strategic goals, including more effective cooperation with America in securing the balance of power in Asia and defeating terrorism in the subcontinent and beyond. If wrapping up the unfinished business of civil nuclear cooperation showcased Modi the problem solver, the PM's quest for common ground with Obama on climate change suggested Delhi was no longer shackled by sterile slogans of the past.

The outlines of a mutual understanding on implementing the civil nuclear initiative emerged in the last few weeks, as Delhi opened purposeful negotiations with the US on resolving three issues at hand—American concerns about India's nuclear liability act, India's demand for a quick closure on the terms of international safeguards, and Washington's support for India's membership of the Nuclear Suppliers Group. If a nuclear deal that satisfied both sides was on the cards, few observers in Delhi were prepared for the developments on climate change, which has long been a site of confrontation between India and the United States. In a city where the virtuousness of India's international policies is measured by their political distance from the United States, Modi promised to 'cooperate closely' with America to conclude an ambitious global climate agreement at the end of the year in Paris. With Obama standing next to him at the joint press appearance, Modi said India's problem was not about resisting pressure form America on climate change. Sovereign India was confident enough, Modi suggested, to handle it. India's real pressures today, Modi said, were about protecting the environment for future generations of Indians from the threats of climate change and global warming. The PM's new approach to climate change is centred on deepening bilateral cooperation with the US on renewable energy and developing cooperation with Washington in multilateral forums. Under Modi,

Delhi's entrenched 'third worldism' is yielding place to the idea of India as a responsible power.

If he chose to upturn India's extended posturing on climate change, Modi outlined his plans for a potentially significant partnership with America in shaping the future of the vast Indo-Pacific region that stretches from East Africa to East Asia. To be sure, promoting a stable Asian balance of power was at the heart of the transformation of the India-US relations in the first term of the UPA government. In the second term, though, the UPA government deliberately began to distance itself from Washington in the name of 'strategic autonomy' and 'non-alignment'. In its second incarnation, the UPA government was also reluctant to deepen maritime security cooperation with the United States in the Indian Ocean. In his statement with Obama on the joint vision for Asia Pacific and the Indian Ocean, Modi decisively repudiated that ambivalence towards the US. The two leaders also agreed to 'develop a roadmap that leverages our respective efforts to increase ties among Asian powers, enabling both our nations to better respond' to the emerging diplomatic, economic and security challenges in the region. If the UPA was reluctant to embark on trilateral and quadrilateral partnerships with the US, Modi and Obama have put the idea of building Asian coalitions at the centre of their regional strategy.

The UPA government justified its American ambivalence by citing Chinese concerns. Modi, instead, appears a lot more self-assured in navigating the great power rivalries in Asia and unafraid of building its comprehensive national power in collaboration with America. Modi's bet on more intensive strategic partnership with America has been reinforced by a revised and more ambitious framework for defence cooperation that the two leaders approved. They also identified a number of weapons projects for co-development and co-production. Equally important was the determination of the two leaders to expand bilateral cooperation on counter-terrorism and homeland security. Of particular interest was their emphasis on 'joint and concerted efforts to disrupt entities such as Lashkar-e-Taiba, Jaish-e-Mohammad, D Company and the Haqqani Network'. Modi's India is no longer whining about Pakistan to America; instead it is seeking to strengthen its internal capacities to counter terrorism in partnership with the United States.

26 JANUARY 2015

Art of the Deal

Modi breaks Delhi's perverse diplomatic culture of negotiating against India's long-term interests.

The Americans, by nature, like fixing problems when they find them. In India, it has been quite fashionable to accuse the United States of being too transactional. The problem, however, is with the fact that Delhi had in the past never been sufficiently transactional. While this has been generic to Indian diplomacy, Delhi's preference for posturing had acquired an extra edge in dealing with America. Over the decades, a perverse political culture, wrapped in vacuous rhetoric, enveloped Indian foreign policy making and made Delhi an odd-ball in the international arena. India would rather negotiate against its own long-term interests than find common ground with others. Standing up against America was considered an over-riding political virtue. Whether it was negotiating on trade, climate change or nuclear policy at the multilateral or bilateral level, defending inherited positions became the dominant foreign policy tradition. Saying 'no' was considered more heroic than splitting difference and making progress.

Part of the problem was the inability of the political classes to continually review and update the definition of India's national interests by taking into account the changing domestic imperatives and the external circumstances. This in turn filtered down to the bureaucracy which revelled in being prickly with the United States. Even a cursory look at the Indian and Chinese approaches to America reveals the contrast between Beijing's pragmatism and Delhi's inflexibility. Beijing fought a costly war with America in the Korean peninsula during 1950–53 which saw nearly half a million Chinese casualties including the dead and wounded. Mao Zedong's own son was killed in the war. Yet less than two decades later, Mao, in a brilliant geopolitical manoeuvre, engineered a rapprochement with the United States to counter the Soviet Union. India, which never had an occasion to fight with the United States, continued to tell itself that the contradictions with America were permanent and offered no room for practical cooperation. If Mao's shift was a strategic one, Deng recast China's foreign policy orientation in more fundamental ways and turned the partnership with America into a powerful lever to build China's comprehensive national power. In recent years, mounting problems with America have not prevented China's leaders cutting deals with America on issues ranging from climate change to information technology.

To be fair, the Indian political leaders were quicker than the professional diplomats and strategic community to recognise the importance of a more productive relationship with the US. It was Indira Gandhi and Rajiv Gandhi who launched the first serious efforts to normalise relations with America in the 1980s. Faced with the end of the Cold War and recognising India's new logic of globalisation, P.V. Narasimha Rao declared that 'sky is the limit' for cooperation with America. Atal Bihari Vajpayee called America as a 'natural ally' of India, and Manmohan Singh signed the nuclear and defence agreements with Washington. These frequent attempts at changing India's relationship with America repeatedly ran into political opposition and bureaucratic resistance. Even when major historic opportunities presented themselves with the US as in the first two years of the UPA government, Delhi found it hard to implement the agreements that it signed with Washington.

Three important shifts that Modi has forced on Delhi are at the root of the PM's unexpected success with Obama. One, at the strategic level Modi has concluded that a strong partnership with America is in India's long-term interest. Two, Modi has sought an end to India's tradition of reactive diplomacy and demanded that Delhi take the initiative. Unlike in the UPA era when all the big ideas for transforming the relationship came from Washington, Modi demanded that Delhi take the lead in seeking a resolution of the outstanding issues and finding new areas of cooperation. Three, he demanded a flexible negotiating strategy that focuses on outcomes rather than mindless defence of outdated positions. Once Obama found Modi can get things moving on the Indian side, it was not difficult for the two sides to deliver substantive understandings.

Modi's transformation of India's diplomatic culture is not just about warming up to the United States. Delhi's new clarity on India's long-term interests and its vigorous pursuit of pragmatic solutions is bound to have an impact on how the NDA government deals with the rest of the world, both at the bilateral and multilateral level.

29 JANUARY 2015

After two summits in quick succession, Modi and Obama had every reason to feel vindicated that their political bet on each other had paid off handsomely. Modi went for broke in finding a way to renew the momentum in the partnership with America, which he saw as central to his foreign and domestic strategies. Obama moved quickly after Modi's election to end America's antipathy towards the chief minister of Gujarat and invited him to the White House. Once they found they could do business with each other, they went full tilt at addressing outstanding issues in the historic civil nuclear initiative, reviving the stalled defence cooperation, exploring common ground on such contentious issues as climate change, and expanding economic cooperation.

With a willing partner in Delhi, Obama articulated the unlimited possibilities for America and India in jointly promoting mutual prosperity, regional security and a stable global order. As he celebrated the virtues of Indian democracy, Obama also cautioned his hosts against the emerging threats to its cultural and religious pluralism. Obama affirmed that India's ability to continually deepen its democracy amidst so much diversity is an example 'for every other country on the Earth'. 'India will succeed so long as it is not splintered along the lines of religious faith—so long as it's not splintered along any lines—and is unified as one nation.' While the remarks generated some heat among the Hindu extremists groups, they were widely seen as unexceptionable. Yet, they also underlined the fact that India's internal political dynamic under Modi will have a bearing on the India–US relationship.

CHAPTER SEVEN

Asia Beckons

One of Modi's early emphases was on revitalising India's engagement with Asia. The prime minister inherited the two-decade-old Look East policy that is widely considered a successful Indian diplomatic initiative. Modi, who had spent considerable time visiting the region as the chief minister of Gujarat, was acutely aware of its limitations. Modi and his foreign minister, Sushma Swaraj, argued that Delhi must do more than look east; it must 'act east'.

Since the turn of the decade, Asia has seen growing tensions between China and Japan on the one hand and between Beijing and Washington on the other. Beijing's muscular approach to territorial disputes in the South China Sea made many of its South-East Asian neighbours scramble for cover. As the region looked to Delhi for greater political and security cooperation in coping with a rising China, the UPA government sounded an uncertain trumpet. Modi, in contrast, has been eager to deepen strategic partnerships in the region and unambiguously claim its historic role as a major power in Asia. Meanwhile, the West Asian region that did not figure too prominently during the early months of Modi's tenure will demand ever greater attention given the importance of securing India's huge interests amidst growing regional turbulence. These columns examine the unfolding dynamic of India's 'Act East' policy and the diplomatic imperatives in the Persian Gulf and the Middle East.

Asia Welcomes Modi

India's Asian partners are cheering the arrival of a potentially purposeful government in Delhi.

If the scale of Narendra Modi's victory has surprised much of the world, one region, East Asia, has enthusiastically greeted India's prime minister-to-be. From Japan to Singapore, China to Australia and Vietnam to Myanmar, Asian chancelleries are hoping relations with India will get a big boost under Modi's leadership. Unlike their Western counterparts, no one in the region sought to distance themselves from Modi all these years. Many in Asia were impressed by Gujarat's business-friendly environment and reached out to Modi. Among the few nations that Modi visited as the chief minister of Gujarat were Singapore, Japan and China.

Beijing surely has concerns about Modi's tough rhetoric on the border dispute and his plans for a rapid modernisation of India's defences. Some in Tokyo might value Modi for precisely the reason that he is ready to make India count in the new geopolitics of East Asia. Many in ASEAN have long urged India to contribute more actively to the Asian balance of power. Most Asian leaders are betting that India under Modi might be a more purposeful interlocutor than the UPA. That is one advantage of signalling strong political will; even those who have differences with Modi in one arena are likely to welcome the opportunity to do business in another.

Although India's relations with the region have significantly expanded over the last decade, the frustrations of dealing with the UPA government, whether it was in the areas of commerce or defence, had taken their toll. Much in the manner that the people of India have voted for a decisive national leadership, New Delhi's partners across Asia are cheering the arrival of an Indian government that they can productively engage with. Prime Minister Manmohan Singh's persistence helped drag India into free-trade agreements with the ASEAN, Japan and South Korea.

But India under the UPA remained a hesitant defence partner. In the first couple of years of UPA rule, Defence Minister Pranab Mukherjee expanded India's security engagement with East and South-East Asia. A.K. Antony, who followed him to become India's longest-serving defence minister, wrecked Asia's hopes for credible defence partnerships with Delhi. Under Antony, the Ministry of Defence turned into a crabby and capricious interlocutor. At the multilateral level, the MoD had neither the vision nor the will to contribute to regional security cooperation in Asia.

For Antony, who skipped important ministerial meetings in the region, defence diplomacy was a burden, not a strategic opportunity. At the bilateral level, requests for greater interaction with the Indian armed forces and civilian defence establishments were routinely turned down under Antony. In a period that saw China, Japan and ASEAN dramatically expand defence diplomacy in Asia, Antony actively diminished India's prospects as a net provider of security in

Asia. The new government under Modi has much ground to make up on economic and security cooperation with Asia.

21 MAY 2014

Dealing with the China-Japan Rivalry

Sino-Japanese rivalry has returned to haunt Asian geopolitics.

If Prime Minister Narendra Modi plays his cards well with Japanese and Chinese leaders, he can mobilise the world's third and second largest economies in accelerating India's development and make New Delhi an important player in the unfolding Great Game to the east. Any reference to the 'Great Game' turns our mind to the subcontinent's north-western frontiers, where Russia and the Raj jockeyed for influence through the 19th century. The context was Calcutta's territorial expansion towards the Indus and beyond and Moscow's march to the Caspian Sea and the Amu Darya. Managing the contested space in between was at the heart of the Great Game. But the Great Game was never limited to the north-west. From Calcutta's perspective, the Great Game was about limiting the presence of other powers around the subcontinent. The Raj had its hands full securing the eastern flanks before and after the 19th century.

In establishing its primacy in India, Britain had to fend off the Dutch power in the 17th century and the French challenge at the end of the 18th century. After the Napoleonic wars in Europe, the Raj demarcated the spheres of influence with European powers in East Asia to Calcutta's advantage. Tranquillity to the east of the Raj was shattered by the rise of imperial Japan at the turn of the 20th century. Japan's military advances in East Asia in World War II surprised the Raj that was ousted from Malaya and Burma. The Japanese armies also drove the French out of Indo-China and the Dutch from the East Indies (Indonesia). Soon after, they were closing in on the subcontinent's north-eastern frontiers and occupied the Andamans in the Bay of Bengal. It needed all of undivided India's resources, military and economic, to defeat Japan.

Thanks to independent India's reluctance to remember the history of World War II, Delhi's political and bureaucratic classes as well as its strategic community have little sense of the complex dynamic of Asian geopolitics in the first half of the 20th century. Modi's emerging opportunities with Japan and China can only be appreciated if there is some awareness of India's decisive role in shaping the Asian balance of power in the first half of the 20th century. In the inter-war period, the conflict between Indian nationalism and Britain sharpened steadily. But Asia's new order was being defined not just by the anti-colonial movements but also the deepening contradictions within the region. In north-east Asia, Japanese nationalism was at odds with Chinese and Korean nationalisms. Elsewhere, sections of Asian nationalists saw imperial Japan as a liberator of the region from European colonialism.

The Indian national movement was, regrettably, divided in dealing with Japan's rise. While there was strong nationalist opposition to Japan's occupation of China, some like Subhas Chandra Bose saw the value of aligning with Japan to accelerate India's independence. While the Indian National Congress refused to support the British war effort against Japan, the Raj deployed nearly 750,000 Indian troops to push the Japanese out of Burma and Malaya. India also became the base for British and American support for the beleaguered Chinese nationalist government that was relocated to Chungking (Chongqing) in the face of Japanese occupation of eastern China.

Seven decades later, tensions between China and Japan have once again become a critical feature of Asian geopolitics. As in the inter-war period, the West now appears listless in coping with the unfolding power shift in Asia. America, which has replaced Britain as the sole superpower, is finding it hard to manage the competing imperatives of engaging a rising China and reassuring a concerned Japan. During World War II, the lack of agreement between Britain and the INC on one hand and divisions within the national movement on how to deal with the Asian geopolitics on the other significantly limited India's political gains, despite its massive military contribution to the Allied victory in Asia. India today is much better placed to deal with the emerging rivalry between Beijing and Tokyo. On the economic front, Modi should eagerly seek cooperation from both sides. Commercial competition between Tokyo and Beijing, for example on high-speed railways, should work to India's advantage.

In the strategic domain, there can be no symmetry between India's relations with Japan and China. If Beijing's growing military capabilities pose difficult challenges to Delhi, security cooperation with Tokyo might help reduce India's expanding power gap with China. Doing more with Japan does not mean siding with Tokyo against Beijing. Here again, the past offers a sensible guidance for the present. India's first prime minister, Jawaharlal Nehru, argued against treating Japan as a defeated power in the wake of World War II. Nehru also opposed Western attempts to isolate China after the communists won the civil war there in 1949. Unless both China and Japan are given their legitimate due, he was convinced, Asia will be neither secure nor prosperous. Modi, then, has a strong precedent to pursue good relations with both Japan and China. The PM should strengthen partnerships with Tokyo and Beijing, each on its own merit, and in the process, build up India's comprehensive national power and make Delhi an indispensable actor in shaping Asia's future.

27 AUGUST 2014

Friends for the Future

As they seek a larger role for their nations in Asia and the world, Modi and Abe know they need each other.

Although Modi could not make Japan his first foreign destination as PM, he has kept the essence of his promise that he would attach special significance to ties with Tokyo. Modi's trip to Japan in early September 2014 is his first bilateral diplomatic engagement outside the subcontinent. On his part, Japanese premier Shinzo Abe is showing up at the ancient city of Kyoto to host a private dinner for the Indian prime minister. As they push for an ambitious agenda of bilateral cooperation, Modi and Abe are both mobilising the past to address the challenges of the present. For Modi and Abe, widely hailed and rebuked for their unabashed nationalism, the past is not really past. They are actively mobilising the past in pursuit of their current goals. If Modi is leveraging nationalism to reconfigure India's domestic politics and its external orientation, Abe is determined to end Japan's post-war antipathy towards nationalism and remake it as a normal state.

As they seek a larger role for their nations in Asia and the world, Modi and Abe know they need each other more than ever before. They are acutely conscious that India and Japan form unique partners for each other amid the current economic and geopolitical flux in Asia. They have one common problem, though. Both are burdened with national security bureaucracies that are stuck with mantras of the past and slowing down the prospects for civil nuclear and defence cooperation. Modi and Abe need to press their bureaucracies to quickly wrap up the nuclear negotiations and lay the foundations for a strong defence partnership. On the economic front, the challenges are more on the Indian side, where Modi must get his domestic act together to take full advantage of the possibilities that have opened up for Japan's participation in accelerating India's economic development. On a whole range of issues identified as priorities by Modi—from boosting India's manufacturing sector to the modernisation of infrastructure, from building high-speed railways to constructing smart cities, from cleaning the Ganga to the development of green technologies—Japan is well placed to become a productive partner. By receiving Modi in Kyoto, Abe is showcasing the historic Buddhist bonds between India and Japan and creating a broader public support in both countries for a meaningful strategic partnership. The two leaders are also announcing a sister city partnership between Varanasi and Kyoto. For preserving the heritage of Varanasi and making it a modern city, Kyoto is a fine place to learn from.

Past and present will also come together in the political engagement between the two leaders in Tokyo. Since he surprised the world by his return to power at the end of 2012, Abe has sought to pull Japan out of extended economic stagnation and re-establish it as a front-ranking power in Asia and the world. For more than five decades, Japan has been content to rely on the military alliance with the US to ensure its security. As it worries about Beijing's new clout, Tokyo is also concerned about America's ambivalence in the new dynamic between China and Japan. While the alliance with the US will remain Japan's security anchor for the foreseeable future, Abe is taking some additional insurance. He is strengthening Japan's military capabilities and preparing it for a more active security role in Asia and the Indian Ocean. He also wants to build stronger security partnerships with many countries in the region, including US allies like Australia and the Philippines as well as non-aligned nations like India, Vietnam and Indonesia.

30 AUGUST 2014

Australia: The Story beyond Uranium

Canberra is a valuable partner for Delhi in stabilising Asia and the Indo-Pacific littoral.

It is not Japan alone that has had a special place in Modi's worldview. The prime minister is among the few Indian leaders who appreciates the value of a long-term relationship with Australia. It was no surprise then that the Australian prime minister, Tony Abbott, was among the first leaders that Modi received in Delhi, in September 2014. The two leaders are eager to look beyond the nuclear issue and lay the foundation for an enduring defence and security cooperation that will contribute to peace and stability in Asia and the Indo-Pacific littoral. The nuclear deal is indeed an important breakthrough in bilateral relations. It is, in essence, about burying the past when differences over non-proliferation issues constrained the engagement between the two countries. These differences boiled over when Australia reacted sharply to the Indian nuclear tests in May 1998. Canberra found it hard to export uranium even after Delhi concluded a historic civil nuclear initiative with Washington that ended more than three decades of India's atomic isolation. There were deep divisions within the Australian political class on allowing uranium exports to India.

As part of its strong and unilateral non-proliferation commitments, Australia had decided long years ago that it would not export uranium to countries that did not sign the nuclear Non-Proliferation Treaty (NPT). The problem for Australia was that the India–US nuclear initiative was about finding a way to circumvent the question of the NPT. While India was not in a position to sign the NPT, it offered strong assurances to the international community that it would not use material and technology obtained through international cooperation for military purposes. India also reaffirmed its impeccable non-proliferation record and expressed full support for the global non-proliferation regime. The challenge in Australia was to get the political elite to look beyond the NPT, understand the value of India's integration into the global nuclear order and, above all, appreciate the broader benefits of building a lasting partnership with Delhi.

To their credit, Prime Minister Abbott and his predecessors in both Liberal and Labour parties have worked hard to overcome internal political differences and get the country to change its long-standing policy on uranium exports by taking a strategic view of relations with India. Once the deal is through, Australia could become an important source of natural uranium exports. The real story, however, lies beyond uranium. Australia is rich in mineral resources and is a natural long-term partner for India's industrial growth. Whichever way Delhi's strategy for energy security might evolve in the coming years, Australia, with its abundant coal and natural gas resources, will loom large in India's calculus. With one of the world's strongest mining sectors, Australia can help India exploit its own natural resources in an environmentally sustainable way and thereby address one of the major current constraints on India's economic growth.

Contrary to the perception that the country is all about mining, Australia boasts of a strong science and technology base that can feed nicely into India's plans for economic and industrial advancement. Australia is also home to a prosperous and rapidly growing Indian minority that is emerging as an important bridge between the two countries. While the natural complementarities in the economic domain are beginning to express themselves, much political work remains to be done on boosting security cooperation between the two countries. For long, Delhi and Canberra have remained far apart in Asia despite shared political values. During the Cold War, Delhi viewed Canberra as merely extending US power in Asia. Canberra, in turn, saw India as aligned with the Soviet Union. The end of the Cold War and the improvement in Indo-US relations set a very different stage for the bilateral relationship.

Canberra's relentless wooing of Delhi in the new millennium has begun to change Indian perceptions. There is growing recognition in Delhi today that Australia, which brings so many independent strategic equities to the table, is a valuable partner for India in stabilising Asia and the Indo-Pacific littoral. Asia's changing geopolitical context—the rise of Chinese power, Beijing's growing assertiveness on territorial disputes, the uncertainties in the US policy towards the region and the emerging fissures in regional institutions—demands that India and Australia strengthen their bilateral partnership as well as reach out to third parties. As Modi outlines a vigorous approach to Asia and Abbott brings great enthusiasm for the India partnership, the two leaders must boldly push for strong defence ties. Besides military exercises that have already been agreed upon, Delhi and Canberra must begin sharing naval intelligence and pool maritime assets dispersed across the Indo-Pacific. They should also initiate joint training and operations with other Asian partners, like Indonesia, Vietnam, Singapore and Japan, who share the objectives of freedom of navigation and security of the sea lines of communication.

5 SEPTEMBER 2014

Between Beijing and Hanoi

The triangular dynamic between India, China and Vietnam is not new.

President Pranab Mukherjee's trip to Vietnam in September 2014 just days before Chinese president Xi Jinping's visit to India might seem like a carefully orchestrated diplomatic manoeuvre by India. Not really. Visits abroad by presidents and prime ministers are worked out weeks in advance. In fact, Mukherjee's visit to Hanoi was scheduled well before President Xi's South Asia itinerary was firmed up. But there is no denying that the coincidence in the schedules of the Indian and Chinese presidents does underline Delhi's expanding geopolitical opportunities with both Beijing and Hanoi at a moment when Sino-Vietnamese relations have seen so much tension.

The trilateral dynamic between India, China and Vietnam is not new. India was one of the few countries in the world that supported

Vietnam when it sent its army into Cambodia at the end of 1978 to end the genocide there by the Pol Pot regime. This brought great diplomatic costs to India, but Delhi was determined to stand by Hanoi and preserve a measure of balance in Indo-China. Beijing, which backed the maniacal Pol Pot clique, chose to teach Hanoi a lesson by attacking Vietnam in 1979. But the poorly equipped Chinese forces that were barely coming out of the turbulence of the Cultural Revolution were routed by Vietnam. India's then foreign minister in the Janata Party government, Atal Bihari Vajpayee, was caught right in the middle of the conflict between Beijing and Hanoi. Vajpayee was in China on a bold mission to normalise ties with Beijing that had frozen after the 1962 war. As war broke out on the Sino-Vietnamese border, Vajpayee cut short his visit to China in protest against Beijing's aggression and returned to Delhi.

Prime Minister Narendra Modi is a lot better placed than the Janata government, whose diplomacy fell between two stools: normalising relations with China while standing by its friend Vietnam. As in the late 1970s, so in the 2010s, Vietnam faces a mounting challenge from China amidst Beijing's assertiveness in the disputed waters of the South China Sea. To cope with the rising China, Vietnam is looking to multiple partners in Asia and beyond. Vietnam has reached out to the United States, with which it had fought a prolonged and heroic war from the mid-1960s to the mid-1970s. Vietnam has agreed to more intensive defence exchanges with Washington and stepped up security cooperation with Japan, Australia and a number of its neighbours in South-East Asia, including the Philippines and Indonesia. It has begun buying advanced weaponry from Russia.

India has been of very special strategic interest to Vietnam. Through the decade-long tenure of the UPA government, Delhi has steadily expanded its defence cooperation with Vietnam and assisted

Hanoi's urgent effort at modernising its military forces. Faced with an intensifying maritime territorial dispute with China, Vietnam has been especially interested in strengthening naval cooperation with Delhi. The Indian Navy frequently visits Vietnamese ports and has been training the Vietnamese submarine force. While Vietnam wants to further deepen this defence engagement, the UPA government wondered how far Delhi should go in backing Hanoi against Beijing. The Manmohan Singh government was concerned about drawing Beijing's ire and its impact on India's relations with China.

The Modi government has signalled a different approach. Much like China, which does not limit its strategic relationship with Pakistan because of Indian concerns, the Modi government apparently believes it can build a partnership with Vietnam on its own merits without worrying too much about what Beijing might think. President Mukherjee's visit might showcase this new approach. India's intensive high level engagement with China and Vietnam could mark a maturation of India's Asian strategy under the Modi government. India is now ready to engage all major Asian countries with each on its own merit. This translates into a twin track Indian diplomacy in Asia: build on the new economic possibilities with China but don't allow it to define the limits of India's partnership with Japan and Vietnam. In defining this new and long overdue approach, Modi is simply emulating the realism of Xi Jinping, who wants to befriend Delhi while holding on to China's special ties with Islamabad and build new partnerships with the Maldives and Sri Lanka.

14 SEPTEMBER 2014

Not So Easy to Act East

Even under Modi, Delhi's default impulses remain insular rather than collaborative.

In changing the name of India's Asia policy from 'Look East' to 'Act East', Modi was signalling that he would be more pro-active and purposeful than his predecessors in the region. To be sure, Delhi has made much progress in reconnecting with Asia since the early 1990s; yet, the gap between the potential and reality has remained huge; so has the gulf between rising regional expectations of an Indian role in Asia and the political will in Delhi to measure up. Modi wowed his Asian interlocutors in Myanmar, Australia and Fiji with his promises to inject new energy into India's engagement with Asia in the economic, political and security domains.

Through his visit across the eastern seas, Modi affirmed that India under the NDA government has entered a new era of economic development, industrialisation and trade. The PM showcased the 'make in India' policy and his efforts to reduce the difficulties of doing business in the country. Modi invited the business leaders and the diaspora to come and invest in India and promised the region's political leaders that his government is ready to wrap up pending free trade agreements with the ASEAN and Australia. In the meeting with the ASEAN leaders in Myanmar, he reaffirmed India's commitment to deepen physical connectivity with the region. He announced the intent to create a 'special purpose vehicle' to implement the connectivity projects expeditiously. He also expanded the scale and scope of India's development assistance to the lesser developed ASEAN states and the Pacific Islands.

That the strategic engagement of the region has acquired a new salience under the 'Act East' policy was underlined by the new agreement for security cooperation with Australia. The UPA government had set voluntarily limits to India's defence diplomacy in the east by deferring to presumed Chinese sensitivities even before Beijing expressed them. Whether it is the intensification of defence cooperation with Vietnam or initiating one with Fiji, Modi's Delhi is willing to do what it thinks is right for India, without second-guessing Beijing's reaction. Engaging the diaspora in Australia and Fiji was also one of the main purposes of Modi's extended travel to the region. As part of a new effort to build lasting bonds with the overseas Indian community, Modi has promised the liberalisation of India's visa policies. Above all, his Act East policy has widened the canvas by drawing Australia into India's eastern strategy and the South Pacific back on Delhi's political radar. Through his visit, he demonstrated an acute awareness of the new maritime dynamic shaping Asian geopolitics and was explicit in affirming India's concerns about the current conflicts in the South China Sea.

All this is pretty impressive. But in the scripted settings that formal diplomacy offers, it is quite easy to forget the enduring problems in India's approach to Asia. The expansive warmth for India in Asia, however, is matched by enduring scepticism about Delhi's ability to convert words into deeds. There is no way Modi can convince everyone at this stage that India has decisively changed course on the economic front. His strategy of focusing on small steps rather than big bang reforms means the progress will be incremental rather than dramatic. If the change in India is genuine and becomes visible, Asia will not need much persuasion to expand its economic partnership with India.

On trade, Modi certainly regained some credibility by negotiating a deal with the United States on trade facilitation and food security. But it is no secret that getting the commerce ministry to clinch the negotiations with Washington was like extracting a molar. Modi too sounded cautious, with phrases like 'balanced trade' that reflect the conservatism in Delhi rather than an appreciation of Asia's rapid pace of economic integration under simultaneous pressures from China and the United States. If Modi does not want India to be an outlier in Asia's trade development, he did not make a convincing case. Modi's promise to fast-track connectivity projects is welcome, but Asia is not holding its breath. They would like to see how quickly the special purpose vehicle would materialise and whether it can change the realities on the ground. At a time when China has come up with ambitious proposals like the maritime silk road, there was little new or bold on offer from Modi on connectivity. While the expansion of India's development assistance is a step forward, Delhi has a long way to go in making the conception and delivery of aid more effective. Inter-ministerial coordination in Delhi remains difficult. The UPA government had backed off from fundamental reforms in how India delivers aid and so far there has been no word on this from Modi. Despite his instincts and intentions, Delhi has much to do before its 'Act East' policy gains credibility in Asia—from the creation of a more business friendly environment to a faster implementation of transborder projects and from visa liberalisation to expanding defence cooperation. The East has its arms open and is ready to embrace Modi, but the PM's hands remain tied by Delhi's political and bureaucratic inertia.

22 NOVEMBER 2014

India's Gulf Imperatives

Despite the region's centrality for the Indian economy—as a major source of energy, market for exports, and as home to nearly seven million workers—Delhi does not devote sustained political attention to the Gulf.

The plight of about a hundred Indian workers trapped in the worsening turmoil in northern Iraq in mid-2014 was a major concern for the people of India. Given India's long-standing tradition of exporting labour and the impact of the more recent economic globalisation that takes millions of Indians on work and business to distant corners of the world, there is always the danger of some of them being caught in zones of violent conflict or major natural disaster. Even though all of these citizens have travelled at their own risk, the government of India has a definite responsibility to assist them during moments of crisis.

Unlike in the past when India had limited resources to bail out its citizens in crises beyond its borders, its ability to respond has improved in recent years. During the civil war in Libya in early 2011, for instance, India evacuated nearly 17,000 citizens. Delhi needs to devise a solid institutional mechanism to cope with what is clearly a recurring challenge. This involves sustained monitoring of gathering crises, warning Indian citizens in time and planning for a variety of contingent actions—diplomatic, political and military—both unilaterally and in collaboration with friends and partners in the region and beyond.

Creating such a mechanism is only one of the many problems that India now faces in the Middle East. As the sharpening sectarian conflict undermines the territorial integrity of Iraq and unravels the old political order in the Gulf, India must end its political neglect of the region. Despite the region's centrality for the Indian economy—as a major source of energy, market for exports, and as home to nearly seven million workers—Delhi devotes little attention to the Gulf. During his decade-long tenure, Prime Minister Manmohan Singh hardly travelled to the Gulf. The absence of any reference to the Gulf in President Pranab Mukherjee's address to Parliament in June 2014, the first written by the Modi government, suggests the NDA might be no different from the UPA. Meanwhile, the Shia–Sunni conflict in the Gulf has already enveloped Pakistan. And the triumph of violent extremism in Iraq will have a huge bearing on India's own internal security. As it handles the humanitarian challenge in Iraq, Delhi must immediately initiate a comprehensive review of the current dynamic in the Gulf and develop an effective strategy to secure India's vital interests in the region.

20 JUNE 2014

BJP and the Middle East

It must look beyond Israel and engage all major regional actors.

Union Home Minister Rajnath Singh's visit to Tel Aviv in November 2014 is a reaffirmation of the Modi government's warmth towards Israel. Meanwhile the external affairs minister, Sushma Swaraj, has travelled frequently to the Arab capitals. Conservatives in India's foreign policy establishment might find the new approach of deeper engagement with both the Arabs and Israel somewhat disconcerting.

Realists, however, would say the government of Narendra Modi is bringing pragmatism and transparency to India's Middle East policy. It's about time.

Consider, in contrast, the UPA government's self-defeating policies towards the region. Yielding to domestic political considerations, the Congress leadership sought to limit political engagement with Israel and undermined the new political consensus on Israel that had emerged under prime ministers P.V. Narasimha Rao and Atal Bihari Vajpayee. The former established full diplomatic relations with Israel and the latter instituted high-level political engagement with the Jewish nation. During those years, chief ministers representing various political hues travelled to Israel. Among those was Jyoti Basu of West Bengal, arguably the tallest communist leader India has produced. But the Congress president, Sonia Gandhi, under pressure from Prakash Karat of the CPM, frowned upon the relationship with Israel. Fortunately, the UPA government did not scuttle the security cooperation that had developed in the previous decade.

The UPA's schizophrenia made India's relationship with Israel look clandestine. Cynics in Israel would point out that Delhi was treating Tel Aviv as a 'mistress'—engage in private but refuse to be seen with in public. The Modi government is having none of that. It has renewed open and transparent engagement with Israel. Overruling opposition in the foreign policy establishment, Modi met the Israeli prime minister, Benjamin Netanyahu, on the margins of the United Nations, during his visit to the United States in September 2014. This has been followed by the visit of the Israeli national security adviser to Delhi in October and Home Minister Singh's trip to Tel Aviv soon after. The two sides have agreed to intensify bilateral security cooperation. Israel's elder statesman, Shimon Peres, was also in Delhi to renew contact with the Indian political leadership. He met Modi as well as

Sonia Gandhi. If all goes well, Modi could visit Israel quite early on in his tenure and become the first Indian prime minister to do so.

It is tempting to see the Modi government's outreach to Israel through an ideological lens. There is no denying the special warmth for Israel within the Hindutva parivar. But the record of the BJP in power has been anything but ideological. While expanding the partnership with Israel, Vajpayee devoted special attention to the pursuit of India's vital interests in the Middle East. The NDA government has begun to do the same. Modi is acutely conscious of India's expansive stakes in the Arab Gulf—as the principal external source of India's energy imports, the most important destination for India's expatriate labour and a major market for India's goods.

The PM is also aware of the significance of the partnership with Iran in securing India's interests in Central Asia and the stabilisation of Afghanistan after the withdrawal of American troops from there. Modi's foreign minister, Sushma Swaraj, has already travelled to Bahrain and is scheduled to visit the United Arab Emirates soon. Modi will, hopefully, travel to the Middle East, early on in 2015. The Foreign Office is also preparing the ground for the first ever ministerial meeting between India and the members of the Arab League in 2015. The stage, then, is set for an open and vigorous engagement with the Middle East under the Modi government. The UPA government voluntarily constrained the relationship with Israel in the name of Arab sensitivities. At the same time it was unable to deepen the strategic partnerships with key countries in the Middle East including Iran, Saudi Arabia and Egypt. Modi must try and strengthen India's partnerships with all the major powers in the region.

9 NOVEMBER 2014

If the Look East policy has enjoyed consistent support from all governments in Delhi since the early 1990s, Modi has sought to inject new energy into India's engagement with East Asia. From Japan to Fiji and from the ASEAN to Australia, Modi has put out the right signals on deepening economic, political and strategic ties with the Asian nations. While the region has waited with open arms for India, Delhi seemed unable or unwilling to raise its game in the region during the UPA years. Having generated expectations that India is ready for a larger role in the region, Modi will have to quickly deliver by concluding trade agreements, implementing connectivity projects and strengthening defence cooperation.

Beyond the bilateral, Delhi will also have to take the leadership role in Asian multilateral forums, where India has until now appeared a passive actor. While East Asia has long been a welcoming arena for India, Delhi faces more complex challenges in the Persian Gulf and the Middle East. If the UPA government did not devote sufficient high level political energy to the region, the NDA government is yet to get its act together in it. Worse still, the Modi government could commit the same error as the UPA government of viewing the Middle East through the narrow prism of domestic politics.

CHAPTER EIGHT

Looking South

Delhi's prolonged neglect of its southern frontier had to eventually end. After more than two decades of economic reform and growing trade volumes, India's dependence on the waters of the Indian Ocean has dramatically grown. The creeping expansion of Chinese naval profile here saw the security establishment in Delhi wake up to the challenges. Delhi has also been confounded by Xi Jinping's initiative to build a maritime silk road connecting the Pacific and the Indian oceans and the warm support it has received from India's neighbours. While the UPA government took many initiatives, its general indirection at home and abroad made its Indian Ocean policy ineffective. The Modi government has talked of giving high priority to the development of India's maritime infrastructure, expanding India's naval and maritime cooperation with the US, Japan and Australia as well as consolidating its own traditional relationships with key island states like the Maldives, Mauritius and the Seychelles. The columns here track Delhi's unfolding imperative to 'look south'.

Sagar Mala: India's String of Ports

The real problem for India is the massive gap with China in the civilian maritime domain.

In its election manifesto released in April 2014, the BJP promised to build new world-class ports and modernise the old ones all along the Indian coastline, as part of what it calls 'port-led development'. The BJP's name for the project, 'Sagar Mala', has evoked, perhaps unintentionally, China's 'String of Pearls' in the Indian Ocean. Over the last decade, China has embarked on the construction of a number of ports in India's neighbourhood, starting with Gwadar in Pakistan, and Hambantota in Sri Lanka. New Delhi worries that some of these ports might turn into forward bases for the People's Liberation Army.

India's immediate problem, however, is not the near-term prospect of China acquiring military facilities in the Indian Ocean. The real problem for India is the massive gap with China in the civilian maritime domain. Out of the top 10 busiest container ports in the world, China has seven. India's Jawaharlal Nehru Port near Mumbai is placed at number 30 and is the only one in the list of top 50. The story is much the same when we compare the tonnage of merchant fleet or the ship-building capacities. If the BJP is serious about generating millions of jobs through manufacturing and trade, it must necessarily focus on a rapid expansion of India's maritime infrastructure. 'Sagar Mala' could be a good first step.

Without strong national maritime capabilities, Delhi will find it hard to either compete or cooperate with Beijing in Asia's waters. Beijing has trumped the talk of rivalry with India by inviting Delhi to join China in the building of a maritime silk road across the Indo-

Pacific. This has put Delhi in a spot of bother. It is in no position to stop China from building up its presence in the Indian Ocean. But Delhi is also reluctant to 'endorse' China's rising maritime profile in what India considers its backwaters. There is only one way out of this corner. It is to build up India's own comprehensive maritime power that will let Delhi consolidate its geographic advantages in the Indian Ocean, build partnerships in the Pacific Ocean, compete with China's infrastructure-building in the littoral where necessary and cooperate with Beijing where possible.

Consider, for example, the Chinese port building activity in the Arabian Sea. For Beijing, port development in the Arabian Sea is about connecting landlocked Xinjiang and West China to the sea lines of communication in the Indian Ocean. China, which is leading the development of the Gwadar port in Pakistan, could also play a major role in the development of two other ports in Iran (Chabahar) and Oman (Duqm). The ports also form a part of China's ambitious strategy of building a maritime silk road in the Indian Ocean. The largest economy in the littoral, India, has watched with some concern over the last decade China's role in the construction of the Gwadar port and struggled to concretise its own plans for collaborating with Iran in developing the Chabahar project. The third port at Duqm, which is advancing more rapidly than the other two, hardly figures in India's strategic and economic discourse.

The plans for Gwadar took a big step forward in 2013 when Chinese premier Li Keqiang travelled to Pakistan and signed bilateral agreements for the expansion of the Gwadar port and construction of an ambitious transport corridor between Kashgar, Xinjiang and Balochistan. In a meeting with Pakistani prime minister Nawaz Sharif on the sidelines of the Boao Forum in April 2014, Li said China was ready to start work on these projects by the end of this year. Sharif, in turn, assured Li that providing security to the Chinese personnel would be a top priority for his government. There have been frequent attacks on Chinese engineers and workers in the restive Balochistan province, home to the Gwadar port. Pakistan, however, is determined to make Chinese investments in strategic sectors as safe as possible.

Chabahar is barely 70 km from Gwadar and is critical for Iran's plan to emerge as the gateway to Afghanistan and Central Asia. While many in India see Chabahar and Gwadar as rival projects, China is operating on a different principle—having multiple connections between West China and the Indian Ocean is better than having just one. There have also been reports on China's interest in investing in the development of the Chabahar project. Tehran is in talks with Beijing to extend Chabahar's rail network to western China through Afghanistan and Central Asia.

Well before Gwadar and Chabahar become ports of commercial consequence, the Duqm port under development in Oman could become a major trade and transit hub of the region. Oman is all set to transform a sleepy village on the Arabian coast into a new Dubai or Singapore. Besides a large seaport, Oman is developing an airport, a special economic zone, petroleum refineries, oil storage farms, dry docks and tourist resorts. Road and rail networks radiating out of Duqm will connect it to other ports in Oman and the rest of the Arabian Peninsula. The greatest advantage of Duqm is that it is located outside the Persian Gulf, where the current trading towns like Dubai are. As tensions mount in the Gulf, Duqm could provide a safe and secure entrepôt for business with the region. As a potential transhipment zone, it would be of great value to Africa, the Middle East, India and China. Rather than complain about Chinese infrastructure in the Indian Ocean littoral, Delhi must develop the institutional capacities to develop maritime infrastructure in the littoral on its own and in partnership with others.

11 APRIL 2014

China's Bases and Places

The question of China acquiring military bases in the Indian Ocean is about 'when' and not 'if'.

That China is seeking a permanent presence in the Indian Ocean through a 'string of pearls', or a network of bases, has been debated for a while. India, however, has been divided in its assessment. Some have dismissed the notion of Chinese bases in the Indian Ocean as fanciful. Others argue that China's rising naval profile is a serious long-term threat to the littoral that India must start addressing now. Many were content to assume that Beijing would remain preoccupied in the Pacific Ocean for a long time and would not threaten Delhi in the Indian Ocean. The world has underestimated the pace of China's military modernisation, the intensity of its naval build-up and the consequences for the Indian Ocean. It is quite clear China has a two-ocean strategy. Although the immediate threats to China are in the Pacific, Beijing is keen to overcome its geographic limitations in the Indian Ocean. More broadly, China's rising maritime profile in India's maritime neighbourhood fits in with the historic ebb and flow of foreign naval presence in the Indian Ocean. Like many great powers in the past—Portugal, Netherlands, France, Great Britain and the US—China too will establish military bases in the Indian Ocean. The question is not 'if' but 'when'.

Since the dawn of the modern maritime age, bases have been essential to the projection of military power, control of critical choke points, and securing the sea lines of communication. Amidst the rise of modern capitalism, emergence of global markets and advances in seafaring, all trading states recognised the importance of powerful navies in establishing access to far-flung resources, bringing them to production centres and shipping them out to globally dispersed consumers. In the colonial age, naval bases in the Indian Ocean were critical for the maintenance of European empires in the east. For post-war superpowers America and Russia, military presence in the Indian Ocean was part of their global contestation for primacy. The end of the Cold War has not necessarily obviated the need for bases in the Indian Ocean.

The US has retained its bases in Diego Garcia, strengthened its Central Command focused on the Gulf and set up a new military command for Africa. France, which had a historic naval presence in the Indian Ocean, has recently acquired a military base inside the Gulf. As a rising great power with significant and growing economic interests in the Indian Ocean, China has every incentive to establish a permanent military presence in the Indian Ocean. Instead of debating China's intentions, India must focus on how to cope with the inevitability of Chinese power projection into the Indian Ocean.

Since the deconstruction of empires and the flowering of nationalism, bases have been politically toxic in much of the developing world. Major powers have learnt that large permanent military bases generate uncontrollable political backlash in the host country. Instead of seeking big new foreign military bases, the US has learnt to rotate its forces through friendly host countries, pre-position military equipment and ensure the capacity to arrive in the theatre of conflict on short notice. The US and other powers recognise that managing base politics is easier in smaller states than in larger ones. The major powers have also learnt to avoid the term 'bases' and talk instead about 'facilities' that are less controversial. That has made it easier for China to proclaim political opposition to all foreign military bases while seeking access to naval facilities far from its shores. As it builds a blue water navy to secure its interests in the Indian Ocean, China needs friendly places around the littoral. India's naval and intelligence establishments are acutely aware of China's determined quest for naval facilities all across the Indian Ocean littoral. The UPA government, however, was unwilling or unable to respond to the implications of China's growing naval presence in the Indian Ocean. The Modi government needs to make amends; quickly.

11 JUNE 2014

The Maritime Imperative

It is probably fortuitous that Modi has chosen his first field engagement with the Indian armed forces at sea.

The commissioning of the INS *Vikramaditya* in late 2013 had made India the only Asian nation other than pre-war Japan to operate more than one aircraft carrier at a time. Narendra Modi, who visits the carrier in mid June 2014, should know that this special moment in Asia's maritime history will not last too long. India's ageing carrier, *Viraat*, is now 60 years old and will have to be decommissioned sooner rather than later. Meanwhile, India's construction of an indigenous carrier is short of funding and woefully behind schedule. Even if New Delhi gets its defence act together in the coming years, India will find Beijing adding more carriers to the first it commissioned a couple of years ago. The rise of China as a great economic power, the dramatic expansion of its naval might and its growing assertiveness in Asia's waters are transforming India's security environment in multiple ways. Delhi, obsessed as it is with land-based threats, has been unable to digest the significance of this extraordinary change in Asia's maritime space, let alone respond effectively. It is probably fortuitous that Modi has chosen his first field engagement with the Indian armed forces at sea. But he can put the decision to good use by reflecting on India's long-neglected maritime imperative.

Hailing from Gujarat, which for millennia was at the forefront of India's maritime trade with the world, Modi may be better placed than his recent predecessors to think of India's strategic future in maritime terms. Modi is perhaps aware that the origins of the Indian navy can be traced back to Gujarat. It was way back in 1612 that the East India Company established a marine force at Surat to combat piracy in the Arabian Sea and secure British commercial shipping with India. Four centuries later, not much seems to have changed, as most of the world's major navies, including that of China, are in the Arabian Sea in the name of fighting piracy. What has changed, though, is the volume and strategic significance of India's trade. While the British Raj integrated India with the global markets across the seas, Delhi, in the early decades of independence, progressively turned sea-blind.

Two factors led India to turn its back on the sea. One was India's choice of self-reliance as the national strategy of economic development. Once India shunned trade, it was inevitable that its maritime vision would blur. On the security front, independent India had to deal with new borders created by the Partition of the subcontinent and China's entry into Tibet. The wars with Pakistan and China in the high Himalayas would freeze the continental mindset of the security establishment in Delhi. It was only when India began to globalise its economy at the turn of the 1990s that India woke up to the maritime imperative. A quarter of a century later, India's world trade, most of which moves by the sea, now stands at nearly 50 per cent of its GDP. India is also profoundly dependent on the import of energy resources by sea. Yet, the development of maritime infrastructure, whether it is building world-class ports or expanding India's shipbuilding capacity, has not kept pace with its growing reliance on the sea. Nor has Delhi developed the two island chains in the Bay of Bengal and the Arabian Sea that give India extraordinary maritime reach and potential influence.

On the security front, India's deeds have not always matched its words. Modi's predecessor, Manmohan Singh, insisted that India's security perimeter extends beyond the land frontiers and covers the entire Indian Ocean littoral. If Singh had the right policy insights, he did not have the political authority to persuade the civilian leadership of the defence ministry to appreciate India's new maritime and naval imperatives. While the Foreign Office valued naval diplomacy as a valuable addition to India's tool kit, the MoD was not ready to fully support the navy's international engagement. Way back in 1961, when Jawaharlal Nehru acquired India's first aircraft carrier, *Vikrant*, maritime power had become entirely marginal to India's economy and security. In 2014, as Modi dedicates the *Vikramaditya* to the nation, the Indian navy must be put at the very heart of India's economic and security strategies.

14 JUNE 2014

Contested Islands: Lanka and the Maldives

To meet China's regional challenge, Delhi needs to reform, root and branch the manner in which it does political and economic business with its neighbours.

President Xi Jinping's visit to Sri Lanka and the Maldives before he arrived in India in the middle of September 2014 highlighted the reality of Beijing's emergence as a major power in the Indian Ocean. While Prime Minister Narendra Modi rightly seeks to deepen bilateral and global cooperation with China in the formal talks with Xi in Delhi, he can't ignore China's growing capacity to limit India's freedom of action on the maritime frontiers. For decades, India had to endure the multiple negative consequences for its national security from China's all-weather partnership with Pakistan and cope with Beijing's quest for influence in Nepal, Bhutan and Bangladesh. Delhi must now prepare to deal with China's emergence as the most powerful extra-regional actor in the Maldives and Sri Lanka. In Malé and Colombo, Xi arrived to enthusiastic welcomes and unveiled China's impressive plans to boost economic cooperation with both countries. Delhi has no reason to object since India too is inviting China's investments. After all, China is the biggest trading partner to most countries in the world. But some of China's economic cooperation in the subcontinent is coming at India's expense. The Maldives, which cancelled the Malé airport contract with Indian company GMR in 2012, has now handed over the modernisation of the airport to a Chinese entity.

Worse still, sections of the ruling elites in Malé and Colombo are determined to play the China card against India, and Xi is happily encouraging them. In both countries, Xi affirmed that China does not interfere in their internal affairs and will oppose others doing so. The reference to India, which has been involved in the democratic transition of the Maldives and promotion of Tamil minority rights in Sri Lanka, is obvious. That China's active political cultivation of the two island states is driven by a desire to gain strategic access to critical locations in the Indian Ocean has been evident for some time. Not surprisingly, Malé and Colombo have embraced Xi's proposal for a maritime silk road. Xi announced plans to intensify defence and maritime cooperation with both the Maldives and Sri Lanka. As Malé and Colombo come close to crossing India's implicit red lines on security cooperation with third countries, Delhi will need to do much more than lodge protests. Nor is it enough to merely proclaim, as the NDA government has done, that neighbourhood diplomacy is a top priority. If it wants to meet China's challenge, Delhi needs to reform, root and branch the manner in which it does political and economic business in the subcontinent and the Indian Ocean.

18 SEPTEMBER 2014

Chinese Navy in Lanka

Modi must now try and make India the defence partner of choice for its smaller neighbours.

Reports that India has objected to Sri Lanka hosting a Chinese submarine in September 2014 are not surprising. A submarine of the Chinese navy docked at the Colombo port just days before President Xi arrived in Sri Lanka. Earlier, in December 2013, there were reports that a Chinese nuclear submarine had surfaced in the waters of Sri Lanka. With Xi making public his determination to expand China's defence cooperation with Sri Lanka and Colombo backing his maritime silk road initiative, Delhi can no longer downplay concerns about Beijing's role in the waters to the south.

The UPA government found it hard to balance India's genuine concerns about the rights of the Tamil minority in Sri Lanka and Delhi's other national security interests in the island republic. Whether it was voting on Sri Lanka's human rights record in Geneva, training Lankan defence personnel in Tamil Nadu, or the PM's travel to Colombo to attend the Commonwealth summit, the Congress leadership simply caved in to pressures from Chennai. Modi might have a little more space than Singh in dealing more purposefully with Lanka; but not a lot unless the internal political equations in Colombo change. For Modi senses the huge opportunity to expand the BJP's influence in Tamil Nadu. He is also conscious of the fact that Tamil concerns are very much part of India's overall approach to Sri Lanka. Modi has begun well by expanding engagement with all the stakeholders involved in the Lanka conflict, including Chennai, Jaffna and Colombo.

India has long opposed the military presence of foreign powers in the subcontinent. This is a geopolitical legacy from the British Raj that was the paramount power in the Indian subcontinent and the guarantor of peace and stability in the Indian Ocean. The Raj ensured that no rival European power would get too close to the subcontinent on the land frontiers or establish a threatening naval presence in the Indian Ocean. As the successor state to the Raj, independent India adopted this position in its entirety. Jawaharlal Nehru vigorously opposed Pakistan's bilateral and multilateral military alliances with the United States. While seeking to keep other powers out of the region, Nehru recognised the importance of providing security to its smaller neighbours. He signed security treaties with Bhutan and Nepal after China gained control over Tibet and offered valuable military cooperation to Burma when it faced the threat of a domestic insurgency. Nehru had also initiated defence cooperation with key countries in the extended neighbourhood like Egypt and Indonesia.

Yet, Nehru and his successors have found it impossible to sustain the twin security legacies of the Raj. India could neither prevent the foreign military presence in the subcontinent nor could it offer substantive military assistance to its neighbours. And as India's relations with the neighbours frayed over the decades, many of them turned to outside powers to counter an India that they saw as overbearing and politically insensitive to their concerns. Initially India's neighbours turned to the Anglo-American powers much to the irritation of Delhi. Recall the 1980s when Indira and Rajiv Gandhi told Colombo not to host American bases or facilities on its soil. The only way of limiting the scope and structure of China's security profile in South Asia is to expand India's own cooperation, including in the defence domain, with all neighbours. The UPA had indeed sought to deepen defence ties with India's neighbours. But it was not a strategic priority for the Foreign Office, the Ministry of Defence or the armed forces. Modi must now try and make India the defence partner of choice for its smaller neighbours. This will take a while, but the policies and institutional framework to get there must be put in place soon.

29 OCTOBER 2014

Focus on Mauritius

The importance of Mauritius in securing the sea lines of communication in the western Indian Ocean.

As a rising China reshapes the geopolitics of the Indian Ocean, India's natural geographic and strategic primacy is no longer assured. As the world's second largest economy, and soon to be the first, China's interests in the Indian Ocean are growing. Beijing must, therefore, be expected to secure them purposefully. China's growing naval power and its vigorous maritime diplomacy are doing precisely that. No wonder China's economic and strategic profile is rising among the island states that straddle the sea lines of communication in the Indian Ocean. The strategic location of these island states has always made them critical for military power projection by extra-regional actors. That the NDA government was conscious of the impact of China's rise on its neighbourhood was evident in Modi's decision to invite all member countries of the South Asian Association of Regional Cooperation to attend his swearing-in ceremony at the end of May.

There was one surprising addition to the guest list—the prime minister of Mauritius, which is not a member of the SAARC forum.

The invitation to Navin Ramgoolam underscored Delhi's strategic imagination of Mauritius as a very special neighbour of India. Despite the acute awareness of the Chinese quest for strategic influence in both the Maldives and Mauritius, Delhi has dropped the ball on both countries during the UPA years. The big question now is whether the NDA government could put the two relationships back on track. Modi's predecessor, Dr Manmohan Singh, had no problem recognising the growing strategic significance of the Indian Ocean. The UPA government activated the moribund regional framework for the Indian Ocean, now known as the IORA (Indian Ocean Rim Association), expanded the scope of the biennial 'Milan' naval exercises in the Bay of Bengal, and launched new security initiatives like the Indian Ocean Naval Symposium (IONS). Delhi had also begun to intensify its bilateral security cooperation with key countries in the littoral and set up new trilateral forums like the one on maritime domain awareness between India, Sri Lanka and the Maldives.

The problem was that the demand for security cooperation with India far outstripped the UPA government's capacity to supply it. Worse still, the lack of internal coherence within the UPA government meant Delhi was prone to score self-goals. As the finance ministry adopted a confrontational approach towards Mauritius on tax-related issues, Delhi could not organise a more balanced and productive approach that took into account India's multiple security interests there and resolved issues through a quiet negotiation.

For nearly a decade now, China has been knocking on the doors of the Indian Ocean island states, seeking greater strategic cooperation. President Hu Jintao concluded his two trips to Africa in 2007 and 2009 with visits to the Seychelles and Mauritius respectively. His successor, Xi Jinping, in September stopped over in Malé and Colombo. Besides laying the foundation for a deeper economic cooperation, Xi announced China's plans for stronger defence ties with both countries. For too long, Delhi has taken for granted its centrality in the Indian Ocean littoral and its long-standing strategic relationships with island states like the Seychelles, Mauritius, the Maldives and Sri Lanka. It is now up to the Modi government to develop a vigorous strategy that responds to India's new maritime imperatives in the Indian Ocean.

1 NOVEMBER 2014

Modi in the South Pacific

Diaspora is not the only reason that took Modi to Fiji.

Prime Minister Narendra Modi's decision to visit Fiji after his pre-scheduled trips to Myanmar and Australia during November 2014 was indeed a surprise. This underlines the new commitment in Delhi to bridge the gap between the potential and reality of Delhi's reach in the Indo-Pacific. The last time an Indian prime minister travelled to Fiji was in 1981, when Indira Gandhi arrived there. Since then much has happened in Fiji and around it. The intensification of ethnic conflict in Fiji between the Indian immigrants and the native populations saw Delhi focus exclusively on securing the interests of the diaspora. The many coups in Fiji and the discrimination against the Indian community there led to Delhi's efforts to isolate the government and lose its broader influence in the island. Modi's visit comes in the wake of the UPA government's decision to begin constructive engagement of Fiji a few years ago.

In the island itself, the 2014 elections saw the strongman Frank Bainimarama shed his military uniform and win a democratic election with the support of ethnic minorities, including sections of the Indian community. If the restoration of democracy in Fiji set a positive context for Modi's visit, the PM announced a number of steps to boost India's relationship with Suva. This included the expansion of India's development partnership with Fiji, improving air links and announcing visa on arrival for citizens of Fiji. Diaspora is not the only reason that has taken Modi to Fiji. Long seen as the backwaters of global politics, the region has increasingly become an important theatre in the emerging great power contestation in the Indo-Pacific. As elsewhere, the rapid rise of China and its intensive outreach to the islands in the last few years has stirred other major powers into action. What began initially as a competition with Taiwan for diplomatic recognition among the island states has now acquired an intensive strategic dimension.

With their vast exclusive economic zones, the Pacific Islands occupy millions of square kilometres of the ocean space and straddle vital sea lines of communication. Some of them provide ideal vantage points for military power projection. They are also important locations for gathering signal intelligence and monitoring outer space activity. Guam, for example, is now critical for the maintenance of American forward military presence in the Pacific. The US also tests many of its star wars systems in the littoral.

For China, which seeks to expand its own strategic influence in the Pacific, limit American military primacy in the region, and gain access to the rich natural resources of the littoral, the Pacific Islands have become an important priority. The last few years have seen China step up its presence through massive aid programmes, civilian as well as military, and frequent deployment of its naval units and the development of maritime infrastructure in the region. China had also built a satellite tracking station in Kiribati which, of course, was dismantled when the island switched its allegiance to Taiwan. China's interest has given the islands more strategic options in their international relations and the means to resist political pressures from Australia and New Zealand. Fiji has consciously articulated a 'Look North' policy and played the China card with considerable deftness. With China raising its profile in the South Pacific, the United States has ended its post-Cold War neglect of the islands and is back in play. Japan too is now committed to doing more for the islands. Australia and New Zealand, which had a free hand in the region after the Cold War, are now recalibrating their policies.

Within 48 hours after Modi left Fiji, Bainimarama was hosting President Xi Jinping. Xi is no stranger to the region, having visited the littoral as vice president a few years ago. Fiji and the other islands are eager for a strong Indian presence in the littoral. They know that India can't match the Chinese, dollar to dollar, in providing economic assistance. The islanders have no desire to switch from a dependence on the West to a total reliance on China. India's presence offers the prospect of greater regional balance in the South Pacific and more economic and political choices for the island states. In meeting all the leaders of the Pacific Islands, promising to make the joint forum a regular affair, enhancing India's economic assistance programmes and unveiling defence cooperation with Fiji, Modi has demonstrated that India is ready to turn its historic links with the South Pacific into a strategic partnership.

21 NOVEMBER 2014

Ocean Diplomacy: Beyond the Zone of Peace

Multilateral diplomacy is not a substitute for a hard-nosed response to the power shift in the Indian Ocean.

Reviving the long-dead proposal for a 'zone of peace' in the Indian Ocean, as suggested by National Security Adviser Ajit Doval during a visit to Sri Lanka at the end of 2014, is not the answer to the new maritime challenges that confront India. Multilateral diplomacy is an important but minor part of a new Indian Ocean strategy that Delhi needs to develop. The core of such a strategy is about building India's own naval strength and expanding its maritime partnerships with other countries through bilateral, trilateral and multilateral means. In the past, when India saw itself as a weak non-aligned state, Delhi believed the nation's security dilemmas could be addressed through moralpolitik. This approach created severe problems for the nation's security planners. When China tested its first nuclear weapon in 1964, for example, India ran to the United Nations, seeking a treaty that would abolish nuclear weapons. India instead got the NPT that only prevented the spread of these weapons. Rather than build a nuclear arsenal, India spent the next three and a half decades denouncing the NPT and proclaiming a commitment to nuclear disarmament.

Similarly, India believed the UN would provide answers to a historic shift in its maritime environment—the withdrawal of Great Britain from east of the Suez after nearly two centuries of dominance over the Indian Ocean. As America replaced Britain as the dominant naval power in the Indian Ocean and its rival Soviet Union sought to compete, Delhi backed Colombo's proposal for a zone of peace in the ocean. Delhi contested the very idea of a power vacuum in the Indian Ocean and bet that the region could build a system of collective security. India asked the great powers not to acquire military bases in the region. It also told Washington and Moscow, 'by the way, don't even think of bringing your nuclear weapons into the Indian Ocean'. If Delhi's strategic innocence in the 1960s was breathtaking, some of its neighbours like Pakistan thought India was being simply devious; they believed Delhi wanted great powers out of the Indian Ocean so that it could establish its own dominance. So much for the consequences of Indian idealism. Irrespective of their lip service for the zone of peace, most Indian Ocean states actively sought military support from one or the other external powers to counter presumed threats from their neighbours. That world has not disappeared.

Doval's invocation of the zone of peace proposal is widely seen as an Indian counter to China's growing naval presence in the Indian Ocean. Delhi has noted with concern the recent docking of Chinese naval submarines in Colombo and watched warily as the Chinese navy matched India's freshwater diplomacy in the Maldives. India's rhetoric about keeping extra-regional powers out of the Indian Ocean was directed at America in the 1970s and 1980s. When India started expanding its interaction with the US military in the early 1990s, some of that rhetoric took a back seat. With China eyeing the Indian Ocean, Delhi is playing the old song again. But that little ditty is not going to limit China's rising naval profile in the Indian Ocean. To cope with the rise of China and the changing power balance in the Indian Ocean, Delhi needs to look beyond the outdated zone of peace proposal. India's ocean diplomacy needs a strong domestic foundation built on more rapid naval modernisation, expansion of civilian maritime infrastructure, the development of the island territories, the capacity to undertake projects in other countries across the littoral and more vigorous naval assistance to other countries.

On the political front, India needs much better political relations with its maritime neighbours like Sri Lanka and the Maldives that are playing the China card as an insurance against hostile Indian policies. Delhi also needs stronger partnerships with other island states like the Seychelles and Mauritius that are being wooed by China with great vigour today. India needs to deepen its military security cooperation in the Indian Ocean with the United States and France and initiate a maritime security dialogue with China. On the foundation of these unilateral and bilateral initiatives, India can expand its maritime multilateralism through such initiatives as the IORA and the IONS. For all this, Delhi needs the civilian leadership—both political and bureaucratic—in the defence ministry to wake up to the new imperatives of maritime strategy and naval diplomacy.

24 DECEMBER 2014

As a historic power shift unfolds in the Indian Ocean, the Modi government has its task cut out in responding to the new challenges on its maritime frontier. The last time such a transition occurred was in the early 1970s when Great Britain ceded ground to the United States as the dominant power of the Indian Ocean. The rise of China as a great trading and military power has resulted in a steady rise in its maritime and naval profile in the Pacific and Indian oceans. It has begun to pose a challenge to the American military primacy in the western

Pacific. While China will be constrained for a long time in developing the capacity to dominate the Indian Ocean, Delhi may not have too much time to get its act together.

The Modi government has done well to focus on military modernisation and put special emphasis on expanding India's defence industrial base. Modi has understood the importance of developing India's civilian maritime infrastructure. His government has shed some of the UPA government's inhibitions on deepening maritime partnerships with the United States and its allies. The Modi government is also eager to step up India's naval cooperation with key regional actors in the littoral. During his visit to the Seychelles, Mauritius and Sri Lanka in March 2015, Modi sought to tie all these elements into a coherent maritime strategy. The last-minute cancellation of the stop in the Maldives, which was going through internal turmoil, underlined the potential problems in India's Indian Ocean outreach.

CHAPTER NINE

Cultural Diplomacy

The international impact of India's soft power was felt long before the term came into vogue in the 21st century. Indian arts, culture and spiritualism have attracted people from all around the world. If Delhi's cultural diplomacy goes back to the Nehru years, Prime Minister Narendra Modi seems ready to lend a new weight to it and combine it with the broader strategy of economic development. Modi's intense outreach to the diaspora also marks a recognition of the role of India's overseas communities in expanding the nation's international influence as well as accelerating India's domestic development. Discarding the traditional Indian reluctance to speak about its democratic values, Modi has begun to embed India's political values in its larger geopolitical calculus. He has also begun to put special emphasis on the idea that India can be the 'vishwaguru' or world teacher. The columns in this chapter explore the unexpected new terrain that Modi has opened up.

Modi's Lexicon

Modi's flair for rhetoric is generating a whole new vocabulary for Indian diplomacy.

Modi's fluent Hindi, through which he engages foreign interlocutors, his instinct for rhetoric and passion for catchy phrases are helping expand India's diplomatic lexicon. During his visit to Kathmandu in August, his play on 'Buddha' and 'yuddha' captured the essence of the contemporary political dynamic in Nepal—where the Maoists returned to the mainstream after a violent civil war. A month later, in Tokyo, Modi framed an interesting antinomy in Asia: the tension between what he called 'vistarvaad' or expansionism and 'vikasvaad' or peaceful development. The persistent use of new phrases by leaders of major powers shapes international discourse. For example, Chinese leaders over the decades have popularised such terms as 'three worlds', 'social imperialism', 'peaceful rise', 'maritime rights' and 'active defence'. More recently, Chinese president Xi Jinping has popularised the phrase 'a new type of major power relationship', which has been adopted by sections of the American foreign policy community.

In India, the debate has unfortunately been framed in terms of English versus Hindi. If the PM feels comfortable in Hindi, is confident to speak extempore and is making a big impact, then so be it. The fact, however, is not everyone in India or the world understands Hindi. The PMO and the Foreign Office, then, must quickly deliver translations of his speeches into English and other Indian languages and ensure their widespread distribution. Some in the East say the rising Asian powers must develop their own concepts for international relations and discard the ones borrowed from the West. That too is a false proposition. Over the last three decades, Chinese scholars have mastered the Western discourse on international relations. Chinese universities and think tanks today are littered with political science PhDs from the US. As it engages the Western world on its own terms, Chinese scholarship has also invested a lot of energy in reviving classical Chinese studies on statecraft and diplomacy. There is excitement in Beijing and Shanghai about building a 'Chinese school' of international relations. Some of them have sought to inject old Chinese concepts like 'Tian Xia'—all under heaven—with contemporary relevance. In New Delhi, Modi and his predecessor, Manmohan Singh, have often recalled the idea of 'vasudhaiva kutumbakam'—the entire world is a family—to underline India's enduring commitment to universalism.

The Institute for Defence Studies and Analyses in Delhi had initiated a focused effort to renew the study of Kautilya's writings and assess their relevance to India's contemporary foreign policy and national security. Much more, though, remains to be done. Kautilya's strategic realism is indeed as hard-nosed as any from the West. 'The strong do what they can, and the weak endure what they must' is an old Greek proposition. India's classics have similarly talked about 'matsya nyaya'—that big fish eat the small. It is not, therefore, a question of East versus West. India must internalise the dominant Western discourse as well as reclaim strategic thought from the ancient, medieval and pre-Independence periods of our history.

Modi's use of the term 'vistarvaad' in Tokyo has got much attention. This indirect criticism of China is unlikely to limit Modi's warm welcome to Xi, who arrives in India later this month. Nor should it dampen Beijing's enthusiasm for building a strong partnership with the NDA government. Before he headed out to Tokyo, Modi was asked about China's expansionism by a group of Japanese journalists. Modi said in response that China is at the top of India's foreign policy priorities. 'It is my government's resolve to utilise the full potential of our strategic and cooperative partnership with China.' Modi also hinted that he is eager to settle the boundary dispute with China. 'I am keen to work closely with the Chinese leadership to push the relationship forward and deal with all issues in our bilateral relations by proceeding from the strategic perspective of our developmental goals.'

The prime minister is telling Xi that the logic of mutually beneficial development provides a sound basis for the resolution of the boundary dispute that continues to hobble bilateral relations. Modi added that 'India, Japan and China have many common interests and we need to build on them to convert ours into an Asian century by working together'. Modi's message, then, is straightforward: only 'vikasvaad' will make the Asian century a peaceful and prosperous one.

3 SEPTEMBER 2014

Religion and Foreign Policy

Modi believes building on the common spiritual heritage can help transform the shared frontier with Nepal.

Many liberals in India have been concerned that the victory of Narendra Modi in the general elections might undermine India's secular foundations and 'saffronise' India's foreign policy. This Indian concern had considerable resonance in Nepal where the democratic and progressive forces are concerned that the Modi government might project its religious agenda into Nepal, which has a majority Hindu population, and empower the ousted monarchy that drew its legitimacy from religion. India will have every reason to be concerned if Modi's personal faith or the Hindu religious organisations associated with his political party, the BJP, begin to influence the nation's foreign policy. There is no evidence of that so far. By endorsing a republican constitution for Nepal and refusing to meet the former monarch, King Gyanendra, Modi has dissociated himself from the presumed preferences of the Vishwa Hindu Parishad and others.

Modi's visit to the Pashupatinath temple during his visit to Kathmandu in August and the PM's offer of prayers there led to much grumbling in Delhi and sections of the leftists in Nepal. But his display of his religiosity in public was never an issue for the masses on either side of the border. They would expect all visitors, especially Hindus, to make sure they have a 'darshan' of Lord Pashupatinath. Asia is a deeply religious place. Leaders from Pakistan and Bangladesh never miss an opportunity to visit Ajmer Sharif when they happen to be in India. Visitors from East Asia make sure they go to Sarnath. Political figures from far and near make a beeline for India's godmen. Indian spirituality has enjoyed a significant global market, especially since the 1960s when the Beatles showed up at the door of Maharishi Mahesh Yogi. Today yoga is all the rage, in both the East and the West.

Does India's constitutional commitment to secularism prevent an Indian prime minister from wearing his religiosity in public? Jawaharlal Nehru, the atheist, had no reason to visit religious places at home or abroad; but our first PM always celebrated the civilisational heritage of India and the world. The religiosity of his successors has spanned a wide range. The canon of secularism does not ordain that political leaders be 'areligious'. What it demands is a clear separation of personal beliefs in God and the formation of State policies. Modi, however, is absolutely right in recognising that cultural and spiritual bonds between India and Nepal provide a strong foundation for building an enduring partnership with Kathmandu. Even more important, Modi is very conscious of the potential of the shared heritage in transforming the economic fortunes of the India–Nepal borderlands. This region hosts some of the world's oldest religious sites, including the birthplace of Buddha in Lumbini and Ayodhya and Janakpur associated with the Ramayana. Modi has long argued that tourism is an important means to promote economic growth and create jobs. Religious tourism, the PM has suggested, could be the basis for rapid economic growth on both sides of the Himalayas. The religious heritage of this region is of great interest not only to the people of the subcontinent but also of the entire world.

24 NOVEMBER 2014

Modi's Buddhism

Modi has put Buddhism at the heart of India's vigorous new diplomacy.

In his outreach to the leaders in the subcontinent and Asia—from Nepal to Japan and China to Myanmar—Modi has projected Buddhism as one of India's bridges to these nations. The PM's overt expression of his Hindu religiosity has been controversial, but not surprising. But Buddhism? Some have seen it as an effort to compete with China for leadership in the Buddhist Asia. Others have viewed it as a fond hope to find a spiritual connection to China. Some point to Modi's personal interest in Buddhism and cite his commitment to restoring the rich Buddhist heritage of Gujarat when he was the chief minister there.

It does not really matter if none of the above can explain Modi's emphasis on Buddhism. What does matter is the fact that the PM has put Buddhism at the heart of India's vigorous new diplomacy. The Buddha has long figured prominently in India's international engagement. As the land where Buddhism was born and from where it was spread around Eurasia, India did not have to work too hard to make it part of India's cultural interaction with the rest of the world. One out of every six tourists to India visits Bodh Gaya. Buddhism has long been an integral part of India's relations with many countries in Asia. Buddhism brought a few problems as well. By hosting the Dalai Lama since 1959 amidst continuing restiveness in Tibet, India has created an enduring source of tension with China.

Beijing's active promotion of Buddhism in recent years has certainly generated some alarm in Delhi. China held the first World Buddhist Forum in 2006 at Hangzhou. It was launched by Xi Jinping, then the party secretary of Zhejiang province and a rising star in the CPC. Beijing convened the forum again in 2009 and 2012. The UPA government responded with a diplomatic initiative of its own. In 2011 India convened the first World Buddhist Congregation. It joined hands with Myanmar in 2012 to convene a conference of Buddhist scholars in Yangon. Just when it seemed Buddhism was becoming part of Sino-Indian rivalry, Modi came along to insist that the religion can be a valuable bond between Delhi and Beijing. At his first meeting with President Xi Jinping on the margins of the BRICS summit in Brazil and in his conversations with the Chinese president in Ahmedabad, Modi spent much time talking about the shared heritage of Buddhism.

Buddhist exchanges between independent India and Communist China ceased only during the disastrous period of the Cultural Revolution. After Deng Xiaoping took charge in the late 1970s, there has been steady liberalisation of the Communist Party's attitudes towards religion in general and Chinese Buddhism in particular. In more recent years China has figured out Buddhism can play an important role in promoting China's relations with its Asian neighbours, including India. Modi's hope that Buddhism might leaven the troubled ties between the two countries may be unrealistic. That does not mean India should hustle itself into a permanent competition with China on Buddhism.

A closer look would suggest China is no competition for India in the spiritual business. Given Beijing's inability to grant full religious freedom at home and the continuing hostility towards the Dalai Lama amidst the restiveness in Tibet, China will always find it hard to realise the full potential of its Buddhist soft power. India, in contrast, just needs to end its prolonged neglect of the Buddhist heritage and begin to invest in preserving and promoting it. Within the neighbourhood, Modi's focus on Buddhism has deeply touched the people of Nepal despite the rumblings of discontent among its habitual anti-Indian leftists and secularists. It has also opened an opportunity for Modi to arrest the relationship with Sri Lanka and consolidate its partnerships in the vast world of Buddhism in East Asia.

Modi's focus on the Buddhist heritage complements his focus on infrastructure and accelerated economic development through the promotion of tourism within the country and across its borders. The PM's Buddhist bug appears to have infected the chief minister of Andhra Pradesh, Chandrababu Naidu, who has sought support in restoring the rich Buddhist legacy of the state. Buddhist heritage is not limited to the contemporary borders of India. A collaborative effort with our neighbours and the participation of other interested countries like China, Japan and Korea could go far in securing the greater subcontinent's Buddhist heritage—from Afghanistan to Sri Lanka and from western China to southern Myanmar.

3 DECEMBER 2014

Delhi and the Diaspora

The BJP's traditional interest in the diaspora has acquired a high diplomatic priority under Modi.

Dealing with the diaspora—people of Indian origin, citizens living abroad, and stateless people who originally migrated from the subcontinent—has been a major preoccupation for independent India. The expansive globalisation of the subcontinent under the Raj in the 19th century saw significant movement of Indian labour and capital beyond its borders. In the decades after Independence, the lack of opportunities at home drove many Indians abroad, especially to English-speaking lands and to the Gulf, after the oil boom there from the mid-1970s. The economic reforms at the end of the 20th century did not reduce the outward flows, but have added new streams to the Indian diaspora.

If citizens' expectations from Delhi were low in the past, Delhi is now under great pressure domestically to respond purposefully to the challenges of securing the Indian abroad. There is relentless pressure from governments in states like Kerala and Punjab which have a large number of emigrant populations in Delhi to respond decisively to crisis situations involving citizens from these states. If politicians understand the new pressures from below, the media accentuates them by 24×7 coverage of any Indians in trouble beyond borders.

More Indian passport holders are living today in foreign lands for work, education and business. According to one count in 2012, there were nearly 11 million Indian citizens abroad. There are others travelling for pleasure. The number of Indians leaving national shores, on short or long trips, has gone up from a little over four million in 2000 to nearly 15 million in 2012. There are nearly 200,000 students abroad. With more than 50 per cent of the Indian economy now made up of exports and imports, Indian businessmen are travelling constantly to manage the huge commercial stakes abroad. There is a variety of situations—ill-treatment, denial of rights, loss of property, hijacks, natural disasters and military conflicts, to name a few—that demand different degrees of Delhi's involvement, from consular support to the deployment of armed forces for large-scale evacuation.

India needs both additional resources as well as better systems to deal with the recurring challenges of supporting citizens abroad. On the resources front, there is no escaping the fact that India needs more officers and staff on the ground and in the headquarters for dealing with expanding consular work. At the level of systems, it makes sense to set up a well-staffed permanent mechanism, say a centre for consular protection, with representation from all stakeholders under the Ministry of External Affairs, long the lead agency in this domain. Three important functions present themselves to this new mechanism.

The first relates to information collection and dissemination. The government needs more comprehensive and reliable data on the movement of Indians across national borders. Effective tracking is critical for understanding the broad patterns and changes within them over time, identifying potential problems and offering better services. Delhi must ensure that Indian workers get mandatory briefings on local conditions and risks in their specific destinations as well as their rights vis-à-vis the Indian government. Delhi must find ways to improve global access to information being put out by the government on rapidly developing situations.

The second relates to the codification of India's rich experience in evacuating Indian citizens abroad. In an important recent study, Constantino Xavier, an international relations scholar at the Johns Hopkins University in Washington, has counted 26 Indian evacuation operations between 1947 and 2003. But there has been no real effort within the government to study this experience, learn lessons and build a more secure foundation for protecting Indian citizens abroad. The new mechanism can draft and circulate to all key departments at the Centre and in relevant states comprehensive reports on how each crisis was dealt with, and the lessons learnt.

The third relates to coordination among multiple government agencies that will have to participate in responding to the crises. The permanent mechanism for consular protection can help strengthen India's regular engagement on consular issues with key foreign governments as well as develop a partnership with Indian communities abroad. It can help structure regular consultations on diaspora issues with interested state governments. It can also better service the standing committee on crisis management that steps in when situations of the type we recently saw in Iraq develop.

The Centre must closely monitor developments in regions where there are large concentrations of Indian citizens and provide early warning of negative developments and explore the possibilities for pre-emptive action. The Centre could also be made responsible for developing standard operating procedures for quick and effective responses from Delhi. The BJP has always taken an extra interest in the diaspora. The prime minister, who successfully mobilised support from overseas Indians during the general election, is well placed to take a major initiative on getting Delhi to more effectively discharge the country's responsibilities to citizens abroad.

8 JULY 2014

Imagining Greater India

An outreach to the South Asian diaspora would be a valuable complement to Modi's strategy of befriending neighbours.

If Modi looks beyond the 'Indian' diaspora and seeks out the much bigger overseas 'South Asian' community, he could find novel ways to limit the contestation between Delhi and Islamabad, strengthen ties with smaller neighbours and reinforce India's quest to promote regional economic integration in the subcontinent. Above all, such an approach could help Delhi imagine a 'Greater India' that is not defined in narrow territorial or divisive religious terms. It could make India, and the subcontinent as a whole, more attractive to investments by the South Asian diaspora and restore the collective weight of the region on the global stage. Few governments in independent India have devoted as much attention to the diaspora as the Modi government has. Consider two recent trips abroad by External Affairs

Minister Sushma Swaraj. She travelled to Mauritius in November to mark the 180th anniversary of the arrival of the first group of Indian indentured labour at Port Louis and the beginning of an extraordinary migration from the subcontinent. Modi's approach to the diaspora is a significant break from independent India's policies, which were defined by either condescension or instrumentalism. If developed further, the policy could resemble the pre-Partition imagination of a 'Global India' unfettered by territoriality.

Jawaharlal Nehru took a legalistic approach towards overseas Indians. He insisted that Delhi's interest in the people of Indian descent should be strictly limited to humanitarian and cultural fields. Nehru encouraged Indian communities to be loyal to their new homelands and was reluctant to engage with their concerns, given his focus on promoting solidarity among postcolonial states. At the operational level, though, Delhi's new elite viewed the descendants of Indian labour with the disdain that comes naturally to the middle class, and was embarrassed by the riches of the Indian merchant communities around the world, which were accused of being too exploitative of the local population. By the late 1960s, Delhi began to frown at 'brain drain' as a new wave of outward migration began, amid growing frustration with the lack of opportunities at home.

Things began to change only in the early 1990s, as India sought to mobilise the wealth of the Indian diaspora in support of economic liberalisation. Atal Bihari Vajpayee went a step further when he called for a more intimate relationship with Indian communities abroad. Yet, the gains were limited, despite the new and grudging respect for successful NRIs abroad and more attention to the welfare of Indian expatriate labour. The continuing obstacles to external involvement in India's development and persistent bureaucratic suspicion of 'foreigners with Indian faces' meant there was little the overseas communities could do beyond lending money at high interest rates. Under UPA rule, even visiting India had become harder, as Delhi tightened the visa system after the 26/11 attacks on Mumbai.

Modi appears determined to engineer a more comprehensive partnership for development with the overseas communities. His promise to improve the ease of doing business, liberalise the visa system and the invitation to participate actively in the acceleration of national development have resonated with Indian communities abroad. The success of Modi's new initiatives will indeed depend on the pace and credibility of internal change in India. Meanwhile, there is no denying the fact that India's internal divisions are fully reflected in the attitudes of the diaspora towards Modi. Rapid economic growth and sustained domestic peace are critical for reducing hostility within sections of Indian communities abroad.

Speaking at New York's Madison Square Garden in September 2014, Modi underlined an important reality about India. If the US had people from all over the world within its borders, Modi said Indians are everywhere contributing to progress across the world. This notion of a 'universal India' applies to the subcontinent as a whole. If the Indian diaspora today is estimated to be around 25 million, the strength of the overseas communities from the rest of South Asia—Pakistan, Bangladesh, Nepal and Sri Lanka—is said to be around 15 million. Like the Indian diaspora, these communities boast of considerable wealth, and are as enthusiastic to contribute to the welfare of their respective countries.

In the last few years, there has been competitive mobilisation of their respective diaspora by Delhi and Islamabad in pursuit of their foreign policy goals. Some communities with real grievances, like the Tamils and Sikhs, have been vulnerable to manipulation by extremist groups. Overall, the South Asian overseas communities have stood for political moderation, regional reconciliation and economic modernisation of the subcontinent. Modi has a rare opportunity to tap into these positive trends within the South Asian diaspora. An intensive engagement with the South Asian diaspora would be a valuable complement to Modi's declared strategy of befriending neighbours.

6 NOVEMBER 2014

Beyond Defensive Multilateralism

The PM must trust his own instincts rather than conform to the prevailing consensus in favour of defensive diplomacy on multilateral issues.

As the chief minister of Gujarat, Modi had travelled extensively in Asia, and his instincts about China, Japan, South-East Asia and Australia have served him well in expanding the scope of bilateral relations in the region. Modi has less exposure to multilateralism. But the PM must trust his own instincts rather than conform to the prevailing canon in the political class and the bureaucratic establishment on the issues to be discussed at such multilateral forums as the EAS and G-20. It was the deeply entrenched negativism in Delhi that tripped up Modi on the WTO's trade facilitation agreement weeks after he took office and reinforced India's image as the skunk at the global trade party. Modi has been quick to see the damage and order a purposeful negotiation to find a solution to the impasse.

Modi has inherited a deeply defensive approach to multilateralism in Delhi. Independent India began as a champion of liberal internationalism, multilateralism and Asian regionalism. By the early 1970s, Delhi's inward economic orientation and third world radicalism made India increasingly marginal to global economic negotiations. Within Asia, India's strategic alignment with Soviet Russia put it at odds with its eastern neighbours, including China, and Delhi voluntarily cut itself off from regional institution-building. Worse still, India emerged as a perverse actor in the multilateral arena, often negotiating against its own interests and becoming a permanent protester. Instead of building a bomb after China tested its first nuclear weapon in 1964, India pushed for the NPT but could not sign it given its unfavourable terms. Turning hostile to the NPT, India campaigned for the Comprehensive Nuclear-Test-Ban Treaty from the 1970s and would not accede to it when the world was ready for it.

In the 1980s, India argued against direct broadcast satellites and transborder data flows, two areas where it would eventually develop impressive niche capabilities. At the Uruguay Round of trade negotiations (1986–94), India vehemently argued against the inclusion of services in the new agenda for trade liberalisation. If the crisis at home and a new wave of economic globalisation in the world compelled India to rethink its multilateral positions, the collapse of the Soviet Union left it no option but to recast its approach to Asia. India's Look East policy was a product of these circumstances. While South-East Asia warmly welcomed India, it has found Delhi's performance in ASEAN and related Asian institutions underwhelming. India found it even harder to keep pace with Asia's economic integration. Congress president Sonia Gandhi was opposed to signing free trade agreements with East Asia. It was only the persistence of then Prime Minister Manmohan Singh that saw India sign trade liberalisation pacts with ASEAN, South Korea and Japan.

As in the Congress, there is deep aversion to trade liberalisation in the BJP. In the name of protecting the poor at home, solidarity with the developing world and standing up against the West, both parties have taken positions that have put India at risk of being left out of the new economic dynamism in Asia. India has indeed agreed to negotiate a trade liberalisation agreement, the Regional Comprehensive Economic Partnership, initiated by ASEAN, but Delhi has shown little enthusiasm to move forward. The US has proposed a more substantive Trans-Pacific Partnership and had no reason to invite India to join in. China has now come up with a wider proposal, the Free Trade Area of the Asia-Pacific, for the members of the Asia-Pacific Economic Cooperation (APEC) forum. But India is not a member of the APEC.

India's defensiveness and the consequent international isolation are not limited to trade but are equally entrenched in other areas like climate change. Overcoming India's political and bureaucratic inertia, wrapped in the rhetoric of high principle and moralpolitik, is a big challenge for Modi. Modi has understood that modernising the Indian economy holds the key to coping with current multilateral challenges. Taking obstreperous positions in global forums does not serve the interests of India, and certainly not those of the poor. Yet Modi's signals have been too weak, and have not really been reflected in the way his senior ministers and bureaucrats approach multilateral negotiations.

Multilateral diplomacy offers Modi an opportunity to unveil pragmatic Indian internationalism built around two important strands. One is to emphasise that India will bargain hard to secure its interests but is always prepared to fashion reasonable compromises in multilateral economic negotiations. The other is to underline that India is ready, as a responsible regional power and an emerging global actor, to become a rule-maker, and to stop wavering between being a mere rule-taker and a rule-breaker.

11 NOVEMBER 2014

Yoga and Democracy

Promoting India's ancient heritage and modern political virtues appears central to Modi's strategy on soft power.

The United Nations General Assembly has declared 21 June as the annual 'International Day of Yoga', following an appeal by Modi when he spoke there in September 2014. This small but interesting step underlines the immense possibilities for projecting India's soft power under Modi. But the extremist Hindutva groups are undermining Modi's soft power strategy with their aggressive promotion of a culture of intolerance and the politics of hate. It is not clear if the government is computing the external costs of lending political impunity to these groups at home. When he addressed the General Assembly, Modi urged the United Nations to support the promotion of yoga around the world. Calling yoga 'an invaluable gift of our ancient tradition', Modi argued that 'yoga embodies unity of mind and body; thought and action; restraint and fulfilment'. He insisted that yoga is about 'harmony between man and nature; a holistic approach to health and well-being. It is not about exercise but to discover the sense of oneness with yourself, the world and the nature.'

'By changing our lifestyle and creating consciousness,' he suggested, yoga 'can help us deal with climate change'.

The Foreign Office quickly mobilised support for the proposal and won the support of 175 sponsors at the UNGA for the resolution on an international day of yoga. The resolution was adopted through an acclamation. The extraordinary support that the proposal won at the United Nations underlines the growing popularity of yoga worldwide. It is only in a few places that yoga is seen as a Hindu religious ritual and viewed with great suspicion. Yoga's international popularity has little to do with the government in Delhi. A variety of factors, including the spread of the Indian diaspora, the globalisation of popular culture and the recognition of its health benefits, helped generate near universal interest in yoga. One can only hope Modi does not introduce the heavy hand of the Indian bureaucracy into the promotion of yoga around the world. Whether it is yoga or Bollywood, Indian soft power has steadily grown over the decades precisely because the government had nothing do with it. Equally dangerous will be any attempt by Hindu extremist groups affiliated with the BJP to claim exclusive Hindu ownership of yoga. This will only invite a backlash, from State and non-State actors, all across the world.

Yoga is not the only focus of Modi's soft power strategy. During his travels to Bhutan, Nepal, Japan, the United States, Myanmar, Australia and Fiji, he has consistently emphasised the importance of Indian democracy. Along with economic 'demand' and a youthful 'demography', he has affirmed, 'democracy' makes India a valuable partner for the world. To be sure, he is not the first Indian leader to identify democracy as central to India's international identity. Soon after Independence, non-alignment and anti-Western orientation came to define India's international personality. It was Atal Bihari

Vajpayee who began to inject democracy into India's international engagement. The NDA government then offered support to the US initiative to develop a 'community of democracies' at the global level. His successor, Manmohan Singh, took a step forward by arguing that democracy is central to India's identity in the 21st century. But the Congress leadership remained ambivalent about lending such weight to Indian democracy and preferred 'non-alignment' and 'socialism' instead.

Neither Vajpayee nor Manmohan Singh were taken in by the Western proposition that India must actively 'promote' democracy worldwide. They recognised that the greatest Indian contribution was in setting an example and demonstrating that democracy is the best form of governance for developing nations. Vajpayee and Singh were ready to offer assistance to those young democracies seeking it, but they had no desire to impose it unilaterally on others. Modi has stuck to that general line even as he highlights the global relevance of Indian democracy. Modi has not let India's democratic beliefs come in the way of economic engagement with an authoritarian China or strategic collaboration with communist Vietnam. He has also signalled an acute awareness of the fact that shared political values can help deepen India's strategic partnerships with the United States, Western Europe and the Asian democracies. If Delhi was hesitant in the past to project its rich cultural inheritance or celebrate its contemporary democratic values, Modi appears bolder on both fronts.

His efforts at projecting soft power, however, are likely to come to nought if the government continues to allow a free run to groups that seek to anchor India's rich cultural inheritance in a narrow and religious basis and infect India's democratic culture with the virus of majoritarianism. The creation of a resentful majority and an insecure minority is a surefire recipe for internal disharmony that is bound to generate severe external political and diplomatic costs in the region and beyond. If unchecked, the extremist forces of Hindutva will not only undercut India's soft power but also overturn Modi's hopes to rapidly enhance Delhi's hard power through a vigorous engagement with friends and partners.

15 DECEMBER 2014

Anti-Modern Hindutva

Resurgent Hindu extremism could derail Modi's development strategy and his hopes for India as the 'vishwaguru'.

In his frequent travels across the world during 2014, Modi has continually affirmed that India can re-emerge as the 'vishwaguru'. His global dream for India, however, is at odds with the deeply divisive religious agenda and the anti-modernism that have been unleashed by the RSS and its affiliates. That India, as one of the world's oldest and continuing civilisations, may have much to teach the world is not a new proposition. Different schools of Indian nationalism—including those who focused on India's past and others who understood modern India's future potential—believed that an Indian leadership role on the world stage was inevitable. Even those who were deeply suspicious of nationalist passions—both religious and secular—were convinced that India's spiritual civilisation had much relevance for the contemporary world.

India's higher economic growth rates in the reform era and the steady expansion of its relative weight in the global system have lent new credibility to the notion of India's international leadership. The example of China has been difficult to miss. After three decades of rapid growth, China is now the second largest economy and its aggregate GDP will soon be larger than that of the United States. Beijing is also the world's largest defence spender after America. The dramatic expansion of China's comprehensive national power has allowed Beijing to now begin reshaping the Asian and global orders. A similar prospect awaits India if it continues to modernise and grow its economy at a reasonable clip. Much of the current international enthusiasm for Modi, like a similar one for his predecessor Dr Manmohan Singh, was based precisely on that expectation.

Faster growth rates of the last decade triggered international calls on India to become a responsible global power and a 'net security provider'. Yet Delhi has been hesitant to accept a leadership role. Many in Delhi interpreted these calls as a pressure point rather than the recognition of India's expanding weight in the world. Modi, in contrast, is discarding this defensiveness and embracing the prospect of a leadership role. Whether Delhi actively pursues a leadership role or not, India's democracy that thrives amidst extraordinary diversity—religious, ethnic and linguistic—is a source of quiet optimism in a world that is being torn apart by multiple tensions.

Modi's hopes for India as vishwaguru are inspired by Vivekananda. The swami spoke of the contributions that India's rich vedantic heritage could make in addressing the spiritual challenges of the contemporary world. Modi, of course, is stretching the idea a bit when he says India's democracy and demography can be deployed at the service of the world today. He also believes the diaspora that has spread around the world and has impressive resources, intellectual and financial, can help realise India's potential as vishwaguru. He reminded his audiences in Sydney in November 2014 that Vivekananda had urged his countrymen to forget their gods and goddesses for 50 years and worship only 'Mother India'. Modi's suggestion that development might be more important than religion is obviously not shared by the extremist outfits of the Sangh parivar that have lost no time in pushing their polarising politics on the nation. He is surely aware that the growing assertiveness of the Hindu right will complicate the development agenda that was at the heart of his successful election campaign.

Given his own experience in Gujarat and the political consequences of the 2002 riots, he has every reason not to let religious controversies overwhelm his prime ministerial tenure at home and abroad.

It is easy to forget that domestic stability holds the key to a successful foreign policy. A nation that is at war with itself will inevitably be diminished on the world stage. When a nation turns faith into a contentious question it invites intervention from religious extremists from around the world. It will also draw into the debate secular forces around the world that want freedom of faith and a separation of religion and state in India. The new push for a Hindu Rashtra, then, is bound to generate many costs to Indian diplomacy. Just when Modi appears to have succeeded in reducing the fears of the neighbours and the world about India's internal orientation under the BJP, the RSS and the Hindu right seem determined to revive them.

Equally problematic for India is the resurgent anti-modernism of the Sangh parivar. Its leaders including the PM have made extravagant claims ranging from the proposition that astrology is superior to science to the one that Vedic India conducted nuclear tests. While asking his countrymen to take pride in their rich cultural inheritance and appreciate its relevance to the modern world, Vivekananda also insisted that India must sit at the feet of the West to learn about improving the nation's material condition. India, then, must strive to be a good teacher and a better student. It must invest in the serious study of its ancient heritage and master the modern knowledge. But if Hindu extremism prevails, India will have little to give the world and be in no mood to learn. Unless he acts decisively to check these negative forces, Modi and his agenda for India could end up being a minor part of the vast collateral damage.

23 DECEMBER 2014

In discarding many of the clichés and injecting native tongue and idiom, Modi has sought to reinvent India's diplomatic lexicon. As in China, so in India there is a rich heritage that can help recast the vocabulary of Indian foreign policy. Even more important, showcasing this heritage, like yoga, can significantly boost India's soft power. India's religious tradition and spiritualism too have long added to the nation's power of attraction. Modi has reinforced the recent Indian efforts to mobilise the diaspora to serve the interests of India's domestic economic development and promote its foreign policy aims. Modi has also been more open than the previous prime ministers in proclaiming the virtues of Indian democracy and its relevance for Indian diplomacy. Yet, the emerging tensions within the country amidst the resurgence of Hindu extremism could severely dent not only India's soft power but also undermine its foreign policy in fundamental ways.

CHAPTER TEN

India as a Leading Power

Continuity and Change

Although Prime Minister Narendra Modi's overall performance has drawn mixed reviews, his foreign policy has won much applause for being purposeful and consequential. On the economic front, many of his supporters, including those in the business community, have been disappointed by the reluctance of the government to undertake radical reform, but political opponents were quick to brand his government and the few changes that he had initiated as 'pro-rich'. The PM's inability to rein in the Hindu extremist fringe has alarmed the minorities and confirmed the worst fears of his liberal critics that the Modi government will usher in an era of communal polarisation and Hindu majoritarianism. The urban youth that bought into Modi's promise to deliver development in the 2014 general elections is confounded by the attempts to impose conservative social values. If Modi was widely admired for his assertive leadership style in Gujarat, he has been criticised in Delhi for not being inclusive enough. All this stands in contrast to the accolades that he received for his foreign policy.

Modi, of course, had the advantage of beating rather low expectations of him on the diplomatic front. He had also inherited a sensible framework for Indian foreign policy that evolved incrementally since the early 1990s, when Delhi's external circumstances and internal economic orientation changed. Professional diplomats in Delhi rightly pointed to the substantial continuity in India's external relations under Modi. The ideas that animate Modi—engaging all major powers, reintegrating with the global economy, promoting greater cooperation with the South Asian neighbours, renewing strategic connections in Asia and the Indian Ocean, and seeking a place at the global high table—have all been India's diplomatic objectives since the early 1990s. Modi's gains, it is held, are rooted in the personal and political energy that he has brought to Indian diplomacy. Further, a strong and stable government that emerged out of the 2014 elections has helped renew international hopes for a productive engagement with Delhi. India's economic rebound at a time of global economic uncertainty and the increasing uncertainty in great power relations have also contributed to improving India's international leverage and lend weight to its voice in the global arena.

The claim that Modi's impact on Indian diplomacy is all about imparting energy to a policy framework he had inherited, however, tends to miss the elements of change that he has begun to inject into India's engagement with the world. Although he has not articulated a coherent set of principles for India's foreign policy, a careful scrutiny of his diplomacy reveals some new emphases that are discussed below.

Economy First

Whether it is dealing with major powers or neighbours, negotiating trade agreements or promoting India's spiritual heritage, Modi has insisted that diplomacy must be the handmaiden of India's economic interests and serve the objective of accelerating national development. This proposition is widely assumed to be an essential feature of any nation's foreign policy. Yet, this simple idea had taken a back seat for decades as Indian diplomacy tilted at windmills on the world stage. That India had a special international obligation for moralpolitik often overwhelmed the logic of pursuing enlightened self-interest. In the era of reform and globalisation, Delhi began to acknowledge the importance of economic diplomacy. But the idea that the business of diplomacy must be a business never acquired real traction.

Modi's emphasis on 'economy first' was driven in part by the circumstances that he inherited from Manmohan Singh. The economic slowdown in the early 2010s had generated fears of an impending macro-economic crisis in the 2013–14 period. Modi wanted to quickly restore international confidence in India's economic prospects and mobilise external resources for the modernisation and expansion of critical sectors in the Indian economy—manufacturing and infrastructure. His economic diplomacy has led to promises of significant foreign investments—for example, more than $35 billion from Japan, $20 billion from China and $40 billion by US companies. These figures must be taken with a pinch of salt, for the investment flows into India will depend upon the attractiveness of the policy framework and the international perception of India's economic prospects. But there is no denying the impressive effort by the PM to spread the message that India is now open for business. Few of his predecessors have spent as much time as Modi in engaging the leaders of international business at home and abroad.

The emphasis on 'economy first' was only in part about making it easier to do business in India and mobilising foreign investments. Modi was injecting the economic perspective into every aspect of international engagement—whether it was urging the diaspora to become part of India's development or arguing the political case for hydropower development in Nepal. Modi highlighted the linkage between promoting tourism, protecting India's spiritual heritage and developing transborder connectivity within the subcontinent and between it and the neighbouring regions like China and South-East Asia. Modi overruled long-standing political objections in Delhi to expanded economic cooperation with China. He also compelled the security establishment to liberalise visa rules that had severely restricted international travel into India.

Confident Globalisation

On the left, right and the middle of the Indian political spectrum, there has been an enduring fear of globalisation despite the economic reforms that Delhi had launched at the turn of the 1990s. The growing gap between the rapid pace of global economic integration and India's hesitant adaptation began to pose a big challenge for the weak governments in Delhi. The new imperatives of global governance on issues ranging from human rights to climate change and internet governance put Delhi increasingly at odds with key sections of the international community. Delhi's default strategy was to resist external demands in the name of sovereignty and take rigid positions in international negotiations even at the cost of looking a spoiler. Playing to the domestic galleries seemed to be more important to Delhi than doing what was right for India's long-term interests.

Modi has begun to discard this defensiveness on global issues. The traditional temptation to posture seemed to prevail when the Modi government refused to sign the trade facilitation agreement at the World Trade Organisation in mid-2014 by citing food security concerns. But Modi was quick to find a practical solution to the deadlock through a set of intensive negotiations with the US. Similarly on climate change, he has begun to depart from the old script and impart some flexibility to India's negotiating position. With President Barack Obama standing next to him in Delhi during the Republic Day celebrations in January 2015, he declared that the challenge was not about resisting American pressure to deal with climate change. He pointed to the growing demands from the people of India to deal with the problem. Similarly on the question of intellectual property rights, he has begun to take a more practical approach to resolving the disputes with the world. On cyber-related issues, India's initial responses seemed to align it along the north-south axis that so influenced Delhi's multilateral positions in the past. It also seemed to drift closer to Russia and China on issues relating to internet governance. Modi is moving towards a more effective projection of India's interests in the cyber domain, including its democratic values and the commercial considerations of the information technology sector that contributes nearly 10 per cent to India's GDP.

Modi has recognised that India can't respond effectively to the new challenges of global governance without a comprehensive internal restructuring and a recasting of many policies that have long outlived their utility. By shedding some of the past certitudes on multilateralism and bringing India's negotiating positions in line with its long-term interests, Modi has begun to alter the way Delhi deals with global problems. But he faces resistance from multiple sources. These include xenophobia on the right and the anti-Western intellectual tradition on the left. There is also the lack of institutional capacity and intellectual self-confidence within the bureaucracy to explore practical solutions to global problems. He will need to expend much political capital and demonstrate considerable managerial skill to alter the terms of the Indian discourse on globalisation.

Regional India

India's turn to globalisation in the 1990s had a positive impact on how Delhi thought about the region. The new outward economic orientation saw India put trade, investment and connectivity at the centre of its regional policies. Resolving political disputes and strengthening regional institutions in the subcontinent, Asia and the Indian Ocean have been the major objectives of successive governments in Delhi since the 1990s. Modi has promised a bolder pursuit of regionalism. His surprising invitation to all the leaders of the neighbouring countries to his inauguration as prime minister in May 2014 reflected the special importance that he attached to the neighbourhood policy. That he was the first prime minister to travel to Nepal in 17 years on a bilateral visit and Sri Lanka in 28 years underlined the new political commitment to engaging the subcontinent. In both places he reached out directly to the political elites as well as the masses. India's neighbourhood policy had long been dominated by Delhi's bureaucracy, especially the Foreign Office and the security agencies. Modi unveiled a much needed political approach to dealing with the multiple grievances of the neighbouring countries.

Modi also underlined a strong commitment for regional economic integration of the subcontinent. With Pakistan remaining reluctant to facilitate progress at the South Asian Association for Regional Cooperation, he made the case for the rest of the region moving forward through sub-regional cooperation, for example, between India, Nepal, Bhutan and Bangladesh. He also began to explore innovative options to deal with China's growing economic weight and influence in the region. The answer to this challenge, he appeared to have recognised, did not lie in opposing Chinese economic presence in the region, but strengthening India's position by a more effective regional policy. He appeared more willing than Delhi's foreign policy establishment to engage China on Beijing's silk road initiatives.

At the same time, Modi was unafraid of contesting China's growing strategic influence in South Asia by expanding regional cooperation with the US and Japan. Beyond the subcontinent, he showed greater political will in raising India's profile and risk some political friction with China. His 'Act East' policy went beyond the strategic caution of the past about injecting Delhi into the geopolitics of the region, especially the maritime disputes between China and its East Asian neighbours. He became the first prime minister since Independence to articulate a comprehensive policy for the Indian Ocean when he travelled to the Seychelles, Mauritius and Sri Lanka in March 2015. Earlier when Obama visited India, Modi chose to make the Indo-Pacific region an area for strategic cooperation with the US. This marked a definitive departure from the traditional policy of keeping distance from America in the region.

Challenges, however, remain. Managing the internal political turmoil in the smaller neighbours remains a perennial problem for India. If Delhi vacillated in the past in responding to the internal crises across borders, Modi has suggested that India will stand by its friends in the region, whether it is Prime Minister Sheikh Hasina under pressure from her opponents in Bangladesh or the opposition forces that rallied together to defeat the Sri Lankan president, Mahinda Rajapaksa. While being generous in addressing the concerns of the neighbours, Modi has not hesitated in articulating India's interests firmly, for example, in pressing Nepalese political parties to finish writing the constitution or urging the Sri Lankan political leaders to seek a resolution of the ethnic conflict through federalism.

India's greatest problem in the neighbourhood is its continuing inability to transcend the consequences of the subcontinent's Partition on religious lines. Nearly seven decades after the division, India's political classes and national security elite find it hard to construct a reasonable relationship with Pakistan. Modi himself confronted these dilemmas as his Pakistan policy went through many flip-flops. If the UPA government stumbled in seizing the opportunities presented by Bangladesh for a comprehensive reconciliation and strategic partnership, Modi has overruled opposition in his own party to express strong support for the ratification of the land boundary agreement. On East Asia and the Indian Ocean, he has said all the right things, but questions remain about implementation, the traditional weakness of India's diplomacy.

Civilisational Identity

One of the significant elements of India's international engagement under Modi has been the emphasis on highlighting India's 'civilisational identity'. Independent India had always celebrated its ancient civilisation and its rich cultural heritage; but they were never at the heart of Delhi's international relations. India's foreign policy behaviour was driven by considerations of territorial sovereignty and other traditional norms of inter-state relations that emerged in 17th century Europe. Modi seems to modify this approach, if only at the margins. As a resolution of the BJP National Executive Committee noted in April 2015, 'Our foreign policy today reflects Bharat's age-old cherished cultural and civilisational values in a more significant and profound manner than ever before.' 'While our approach is determined by the imperatives of the globalised world,' the resolution added, 'it is also rooted in our inheritance of a timeless tradition of intellectual and economic engagement through peaceful coexistence.' It praised Modi for drawing global attention to India's cultural traditions 'in a manner that befits this oldest civilisation in the world.'

Modi has been uninhibited in the display of personal religiosity during foreign travels. He has turned to India's ancient wisdom to frame contemporary foreign policy interests and re-invoked the claim that India can and must be a 'vishwaguru' (a teacher for the world). He launched a special campaign to promote yoga around the world. His outreach to the diaspora, the 'children of Mother India', had a strong cultural dimension. It is important to note that Modi's India is not alone in invoking the past in pursuing political objectives in the present. Cultural revivalism has been a major political tool for the Chinese Communist Party since the turn of the 21st century. Confucius, reviled in Mao's time as representing the decrepit feudal ideology, is now revered in China. Academics are digging into the past to construct a 'Chinese school' of international relations. Restoring past glory is very much a part of President Xi Jinping's 'Chinese dream'.

Revivalism might help consolidate nationalism in China, but is deeply divisive in India. The efforts of the Hindu right to promote a new identity for India has generated much political heat. Hindu revivalism has also reinforced impulses of anti-modernism and xenophobia. It has created a permissive environment to impose one particular set of values on a diverse population. The impact of this new dynamic is not limited to India's domestic politics but will eventually affect its international relations. Obama's public reference to the dangers of deepening religious and cultural divide in India during his visit to Delhi hinted at the kind of negative international reaction to the construction of a civilisational identity for India that is bitterly contested within the nation. To be sure, India needs to invest much in recovering, preserving and promoting all of India's cultural heritage. There is also a strong case to deploy India's rich inheritance for diplomatic and strategic purposes. But any attempt at constructing India's civilisational identity on a narrow basis will be doubly counterproductive—at home and abroad.

A Leading Power?

Beyond the civilisational construct for Delhi's foreign policy, Modi has come up with what could be an interesting way of defining a new international identity for India—'a leading power'. Modi told the annual gathering of Indian envoys in Delhi during February 2015 that 'the present global environment represents a rare opportunity, when the world is keen to embrace India'. Urging the envoys to shed their old mindsets, he asked them 'to use this unique opportunity to help India position itself in a leading role, rather than just a balancing force, globally'. Since then the idea of a 'leading power' has come to represent the definitive reframing of India's foreign policy under Modi. Although the idea of India as a 'leading power' has not been fleshed out in great detail, its essence is not difficult to glean.

For one, it recognises that India's absolute weight in the international system has grown significantly since it embarked on the path of economic reform and globalisation. In 2014, it was the world's third largest economy (measured in terms of purchasing power parity) and could win that rank for the size of GDP in nominal terms by 2030. Its defence budget was the eighth biggest in the world and its military manpower was the world's second largest. These aggregate capabilities do not square with the persistent defensiveness of Delhi. Modi is therefore suggesting that Delhi must unlearn some of the ideas that guided its international policies in the 20th century and develop new concepts for India's international engagement.

Among the ideas that Modi would like the foreign policy establishment to forget are non-alignment and strategic autonomy. Neither the BJP election manifesto nor Modi since the 2014 election have used either term to describe India's foreign policy. The emphasis instead is on India taking its rightful place in the world as a great power. Although Nehru saw India emerging as one of the five great powers of the international system, Delhi increasingly saw itself as a weak developing state that must resist the attempts by great powers to limit its freedom of action. But if India were to be viewed as a great power contributing to the maintenance of the regional and global order, the focus is bound to move away from non-alignment. Modi is also acutely conscious of the fact that India's economy is locked in a profound interdependence with the rest of the world, with nearly 50 per cent of India's GDP linked to imports and exports. This interdependence demands that India shape its external environment rather than seek 'autonomy' from it. If strategic autonomy was a defensive concept, Modi is staking claim for 'strategic influence' on the world beyond India's border.

Modi appears conscious of the fact that the unfolding shift in global economic and military balance makes India an attractive partner to all the other powers. Delhi is therefore well positioned to accelerate

India's economic development and strengthen its military capabilities in collaboration with other powers. India can take advantage of its unique position in the international arena only if it reaches out to all the powers, including America and China. Under the UPA government, India held back from deeper strategic cooperation with America in the name of 'strategic autonomy'. Despite the positive evolution of India's relationship with the US since the 1990s, the policy elite in Delhi remain deeply ambivalent about constructing a strategic partnership with America. It is this wariness towards the West that really animates the Indian concept of 'strategic autonomy' and its quest for a 'multipolar' world. Modi has made it clear that he is not burdened by the Indian elite's anti-Americanism of the past.

Modi appreciates the fact that partnership with the West is critical for rapid development of India's comprehensive national power. In the past, India was deeply conscious of the asymmetry of power and was afraid to engage. Therefore it continually sought to limit the role of the West in Asia and the world. Modi, in contrast, appears confident that India has no reason to be a balancing power against the West and is self-assured enough to believe that a rising India can develop terms of engagement with the West that are mutually beneficial. Although Delhi talks of strategic partnership with Beijing, India has been reluctant to embark on a substantive economic engagement with China. A closer partnership with the West does not mean, Modi has insisted, that India would become a junior partner for America in balancing China. He demonstrated special personal warmth towards President Xi Jinping and is determined to expand economic cooperation with China despite the tensions on the border and growing regional competition.

Modi's talk of India as a leading power is not empty rhetoric. He has matched that ambition with leadership at home by discarding foreign policy populism that had afflicted all major parties in India for many decades. Unlike Manmohan Singh, who ceded a veto to every single department in the government on diplomacy, Modi forced the bureaucracy to abandon long-held positions, and seek pragmatic solutions to problems at hand. He has also put politics back in command of foreign and national security policies. Whether it was in removing roadblocks to cooperation with Nepal, rejuvenating SAARC, resolving the nuclear liability issue with the US, changing the terms of the Rafale aircraft negotiations with France, the decision to develop sensitive infrastructure in the Seychelles and Mauritius, or injecting flexibility into India's negotiating positions on trade and climate change, Modi has demonstrated a decisiveness that had been conspicuously absent during the UPA rule.

The Strategic Sweet Spot

The government of India's annual economic survey presented in February 2015 talked about the prospect for sustained high economic growth rates over an extended period of time thanks to a number of developments, including the emergence of a strong political leadership at home and favourable international circumstances. The same could be said about India's geopolitics. Modi's India entered a virtuous circle with a rare opportunity to leverage the international situation to accelerate Delhi's rise and the nation's growing capabilities to reshape the international system. Acutely conscious of the historic moment in India's international evolution, Modi did not hesitate to dispense with conventional wisdom on India's foreign policy, including that in his own party. He crafted a new vocabulary for India's foreign policy and began to move India away from its traditional defensive approach to international affairs.

The idea of India as a leading power finds much resonance around the world. Within the subcontinent, India's smaller neighbours have waited long for India to take the lead on regional economic integration and devote greater attention to resolve long-standing bilateral issues. In the extended neighbourhood of Asia and the Indian Ocean, there has been a clamour for a larger Indian role in stabilising the regional balance of power at a moment of great turbulence to the east and west of India. The major powers want to widen the areas of cooperation with Delhi. In the multilateral arena, there is a growing recognition that the problems of global governance can't be addressed without a more effective Indian contribution. As expectations from Modi's India rise in the regional and international arena, there is no denying the persistent scepticism. India has disappointed itself and the world in the past. India's internal problems, the inertia of its national security establishment, and the reluctance of its political class to think about the world in strategic terms do threaten to slow the pace of India's transition to a leadership role. Yet, it is worth noting, the reorientation of India's international role might well have acquired an irreversible momentum under Narendra Modi.

Index

About the Author

C. Raja Mohan, a leading commentator on international affairs, has long offered deep insights into India's engagement with the world. *Foreign Policy* magazine named him one of the world's top hundred thinkers in 2009. He is a contributing editor for *The Indian Express* and a distinguished fellow at the Observer Research Foundation, Delhi. He is also associated with the Carnegie Endowment for International Peace, Washington, DC; Institute of South Asian Studies, Singapore; and the Lowy Institute, Sydney. He has served on India's National Security Advisory Board. His earlier books include *Crossing the Rubicon: The Shaping of India's New Foreign Policy*; *Impossible Allies: India, the United States and the Global Nuclear Order*; and *Samudra Manthan: Sino-Indian Rivalry in the Indo-Pacific.*